To the people of Ukra

Acknowledgements

A special thank you to Adam Davidson, Yulia Koshova, Oleg Dmitriev, Sunflower Scotland (the charity for Ukraine based in Edinburgh) and my family.

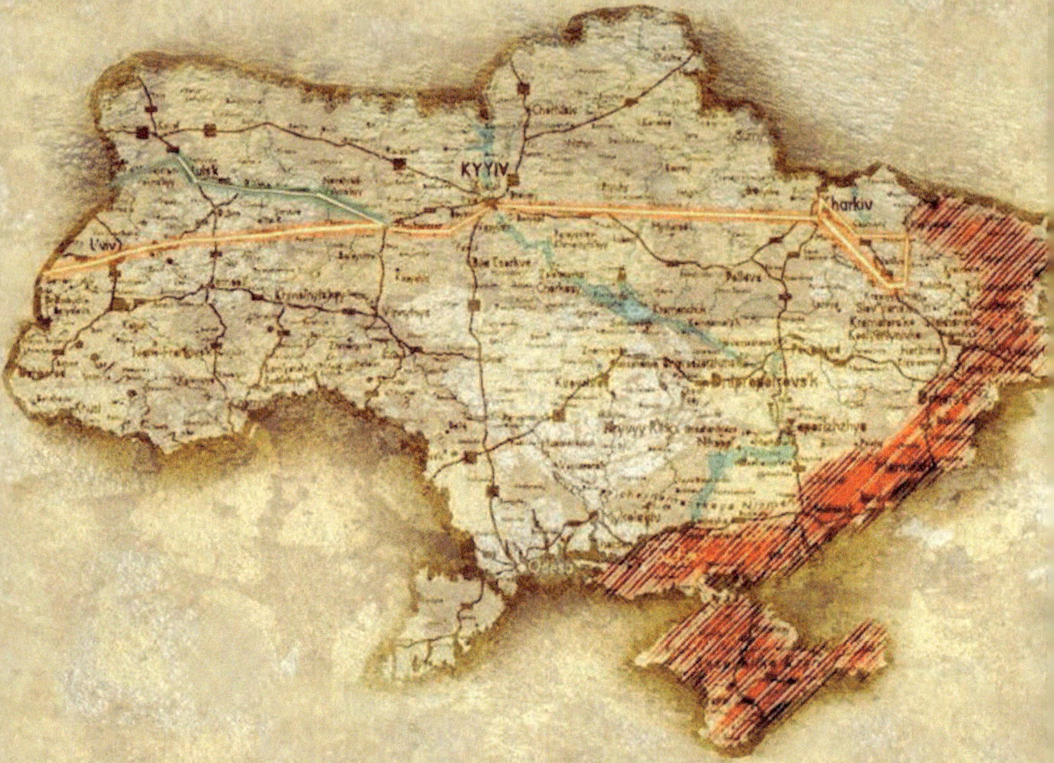
KYYIV
Kharkiv
L'viv

Foreword

When I first met Oleg for a drink after he had returned from Ukraine for the second time, and I said I would like to come with him to help and potentially write a short book on our experiences, he shook his head.

'It is not right to discuss such things when we are here. You must see. I cannot explain. To talk of this when we are here is not correct.'

Having since been there and written a short book on our experiences, I couldn't agree more.

Before leaving for Ukraine, my idea of writing this was at most embryonic. I had no idea what we would encounter or what I could write about, and whether I would be able to write anything at all based on our journey. It became quite apparent to me after a day or two that I had no choice. It became a compulsion. The information was too terrific. The ideas shared and the truths learned, impossible to ignore. The people we met and their stories, too worthy of being remembered. So it was that I sat in the front seat for much of the journey with my notepad and pen.

In some ways, I feel that writing was my shield. If I had borne witness and not written this, perhaps it would have affected me more profoundly than it has, which is saying something. People asked me so often when I returned. 'How was Ukraine?' I have yet to find a way to answer that question. I think writing this book was my way of doing so.

How was Ukraine? Ukraine was many things. My only hope in writing this is that I do the people and the country justice. This was my main dilemma. I have tried to give as detailed an account as I can and tried to go deeper where possible.

Certainly, it is an experience I will never forget.

When I was preparing to leave, a British man was killed in Kharkiv Oblast, and subsequently, others perished that volunteered to go and offer what they could. Many of these people gave a great deal more than I have and have nothing but my absolute respect.

These news stories did nothing to calm the fears of my family and friends before I left. I owe them all great thanks for not making my departure harder. It would have been a heinous burden to have carried to Ukraine, and I appreciate the burden they carried while I was there. Special thanks to my parents and in-laws and my wonderful wife, Viktoria, for being supportive and understanding.

To Adam Davidson for his contributions to the work. For the front cover, back cover, and map. Yulia Koshova for her brilliant artwork, which helped inspire the front cover. She is truly a great artist. To my friends who helped brutally critique my first couple of drafts of the book and told me to keep my authorial comments to myself.

To Oleg Dmitriev, who I will forever be bound to after this unique trip. Who helped keep me safe and who drove an unreasonable number of miles.

To the whole of the Sunflower Scotland team and their donors, who are doing remarkable charity work in Ukraine. The money is going to good use.

Above all, however, I give my thanks to the Ukrainian people. You have my eternal gratitude and respect.

You fight for us all.

You suffer for us all.

May you endure.

All proceeds made from this book will go towards humanitarian aid in Ukraine.

Please visit www.sunflowerscotland.co.uk to donate today.

Slava Ukraini

November 8th

BUDOMIERCZ

09:13

The sound of laughter and running skip off the surface of the vacant lot and through Oleg's window as a young woman and man in army fatigues run around the outhouse. Some of the border guards are already lined up. They hasten toward the roll call.

We are the only car at the crossing. It has taken us a little more than twenty minutes to get to the fourth and final check.

'Shit,' Oleg says.

'Huh?'

'Ahh, good kind of shit. The last time I was here in August, there were lots of cars. We might have made Kyiv after all.'

A window slides open, and a woman's head appears. Her stolid face peers out at us. It is not the face of a Ukrainian. Pole. Or any other nationality. It is the universal face of the bureaucrat. Utterly expressionless.

'How heavy is the cargo?'

'560 kilograms,' Oleg replies unflinchingly.

Her window slams shut again. We are given no indication of whether this answer is satisfactory or not.

Eventually, our passports are returned to us. Oleg is given back his paperwork, and we enter Ukraine. Oleg is still shaking his head.

'We could have made Kyiv. Who would have thought it.'

After a short road, we reach a roundabout. Oleg pulls over while he consults and, not for the last time during our trip, berates the GPS system. While we are pulled over, a man in a car with Polish number plates calls over to us in Russian.

'Spasiba,' the man shouts over when Oleg is finished giving him directions.

'Here we are in Western Ukraine with someone speaking to us in Russian. Here we see the Lingua Franca. Poor oppressed Russian speakers.' Oleg smiles tightly and turns to me.

'What you see with your eyes is true. If you don't see it, then don't believe it.'

Out of the corn crops of Poland, the broken golden stems are left behind and onto the bare black earth where the sunflowers have been harvested. Miles and miles of fields, on a scale, like many things, that must be witnessed to be understood.

'This is the first thing. It is important. When we are in Ukraine, I want you to pay attention to the quality of life,' Oleg says.

As we skirt around Lviv, fine houses spring up in the countryside. Two storeys high, with tall fences and imposing gates. Then he points at the billboards that line the sides of the motorway and quickly translates.

'This one is about new apartments. This one advertises a spa. A new amusement park. Builders that do facades for houses. Pieces of land for sale. These are not old; many have been put up since the start of the war.

The point is you don't cross over the border to dead bodies. This is a perception in the West. All of Ukraine filled with dead bodies and people on their knees with their hands out like beggars. This is not the case. Business is still going on. The country is still working.'

With perfect timing, we drive into a beautiful little village. There is a man-made lake with boats tied to the numerous piers. We stop so that I could exchange some of my money in a small shop on the high street. The shop is packed with products and people. The queue for the checkout is ten deep. As Oleg speaks to the woman in the small bureau de change booth, I look around a bit.

There are vegetables neatly stacked on display. Meat. Fish. Cheese. This I wasn't expecting. When we leave the shop, I comment on the abundant selection, something I might struggle to find in a shop back in Edinburgh.

'We can't keep treating Ukraine like it's a third-world country when clearly it is not,' Oleg says, 'this is not a failed state.'

We see far more of Ukraine than we planned to on the drive to Zhytomyr. I am quietly pleased by this. We go through little villages, turned golden by the autumn, in what, during a different time and situation, would have been a scenic route. The Ukrainian flags blow in the wind wherever we pass through. In some of the hamlets, I think the flags may outnumber the populace. Alongside the yellow and blue flies another flag of red and black. It is the patriot's flag. Oleg explains that red is for the blood of the country, and black is for the soil.

'I thought we might have seen some of the war already.'

'Every part of Ukraine has suffered just in different ways. Here it is not so visible, but in Lviv Oblast, they have lost people, and they have had to learn to live with the consequences of war.'

Sometime later, a graveyard passes us. Oleg gestures towards them, 'the graves with the Ukrainian flags next to them are for soldiers who have died in the conflict.'

There are quite a few flags.

Just outside Brody, we stop at a gas station. It is one of the many Okko's and Wog's we stop at, and I'd swear by either of them. Oleg is smiling as we go in.

'You've noticed the roads, I hope, by now? Maybe Edinburgh council should send some people here, get shown how to make roads properly. But the gas stations…you like salmon?'

I sit at the table at the gas station with a salmon steak and salad and fresh bread. When we have finished eating, I go out for a cigarette where I 'chat' with a man called Bogdan. We quickly realise we are at a lingual impasse when it takes two minutes to trade names.

'Teplo,' he says, pointing at the sky.

'Sun?'

'Yes.'

We smoke in near silence after, but he noticed the van with its stickers for Sunflower Scotland on it when we pulled in. He points to it and gives me a smile and a firm handshake.

We get back in the van and onto the E40 for the final three hundred kilometres to Zhytomyr. Oleg is on his fourth day straight of long-distance driving. Three hundred kilometres, he says, is nothing at all.

Bogdan is right. It is a gorgeous day. Oleg and I chat on and off. Other times I stare out of the window at the sweeping landscape. The bare trunks of the pine trees and the silver of the birches. The miles and miles of farmland.

This ride gives me an odd feeling. Driving along the motorway, I almost feel like I am on holiday. If I had been dropped into this car with no explanation and given no indicators of my whereabouts, I could easily believe we were in Germany, France, and Belgium. Anywhere but a warzone.

An hour from Zhytomyr, we discuss Britain's response to the Ukrainian war.

'It was a lot,' Oleg says, sighing and drumming his fingers on the steering wheel. 'The problem with the house a Ukrainian scheme wasn't whether it was enough or not. Think of it this way.

What if you don't have access to a computer? What if you aren't computer literate? What if your house is destroyed? What if you have no internet? What if you have no electricity? What if you have limited English? Good luck finding a host. What if you don't have the money to leave?'

With each point he makes, the index finger on his hand shoots up. It's a checklist of parameters that many Ukrainians cannot tick off.

'Most of the people who applied were the ones who could. They are from the cities and bigger towns. They have enough affluence to have disposable income. They are likely educated, and some can speak English very well. But the hopeless, those who need help, are often incapable of having their voices heard. Or they have no choice but silence. Those that are heard are often the ones who need it less.'

'Are you angry?'

'Yes, a little. Not with Ukrainians. This is normal. The country is at war. They see an opportunity for a better life. I would do the same, I think. I am also sad. The worst hit people. What was their crime? Where they were born? How poor they were? This is not the Ukrainians' fault, but it is not right. It's a triage ward, David. But instead of helping the people who have had their legs blown off, we're helping the people that have black eyes. And we're still doing it now.

The Scottish Government set up a Ukrainian Response Team, and not one of them has been to Ukraine. How can this be?' He points at me, 'no disrespect, but a waiter is about to know more about the situation than people employed to deal with it. I contacted them. I told them I had been there. I offer them my insight. I tell them I am happy to help. I recommend they send people to help assess. It was useless. You know what they told me. They quoted me the government line. The advice is do not travel. So, we will not go against that to support individuals or small-scale NGOs. Clearly, they are happy to be blind. My question is this: how can a response evolve without education? And how can you help with a humanitarian crisis like this and hope to avoid any danger?'

I mull this over in my head as we drive on.

I remember meeting Oleg back in August. We had met many months previous when the restaurant I work in had held fundraisers, and I had helped fill a huge truck that was going to Ukraine. When we met, and I reminded him of this, he facepalmed and looked mildly distraught. I asked him why this upset him.

'We filled it with food and clothes. This was a mistake.'

When I asked him how he knew it was a mistake, the answer was quite simple. He had gone to Ukraine. He had been told that the food and the clothes being sent were destroying the local economy. With the Ukrainian economy on course to retract by thirty percent, the last thing it needs is free items. Not only this, but Oleg tells me that many goods being sent are being sold in Ukraine for profit.

The Modus Operandi of Sunflower Scotland has changed ever since. Everything that they take to the villages and towns is bought in Ukraine. This is how evolution looks. It often starts with a mistake.

'I think some people are happier when charity is convenient. All these details and things to consider. Nuisance.'

'You think they should have vetted people better?'

'Vetted at all. I have an idea. You give each designated area, say 1,000 people, something like this, say Kharkiv Oblast, Kherson Oblast,' he motions with his hand, 'etcetera.

If you are in a warzone, you have had your house destroyed and been through the trauma of frontline living; you should have priority. We took the fittest. We took the most able. A lot of the time, this was the case. Anyway. You will see. You will see.'

I contemplated this point. 'Do you think we might have made Ukraine weaker?'

'Ooo. Careful. This is controversial.'

ZHYTOMYR

19:06

Our passports are checked on the way into the city; the soldier clicks on his flashlight. My passport first, Oleg's second. It is better this way. Oleg was born in Moscow. He asks a couple of questions, to which Oleg replies. He passes our passports back and lets us through. This little ritual I get very well acquainted with during my time in Ukraine.

Zhytomyr is pitch black; the lamps are extinguished. Blackout. The sun is long gone, and we twist through the narrow streets carefully. I get little glimpses of the city, half-seen ancient churches, and the shops that you could take for being derelict.

'Curfew begins at 00:00 and ends at 06:00.'

Says the sign on the hotel door. We are checked in by Veronika, who speaks to us in perfect English. She reiterates the information we have just read on the sign before directing us toward the restaurant.

'Would you like to have a table for this evening?'

Half an hour later, our starters arrived. Two bowls of borscht, with little ramekins of lard and sour cream. Oleg has a duck salad for main. I have a chicken caesar salad. We both have a glass of wine produced in a local vineyard.

I dab my lips with the freshly pressed fabric napkin and look around at the fine layout and décor while waist-coated waiters and waitresses whirl by to serve other customers.

It all feels surreal, as if it is an act. A show that I am being presented with.

I consider myself well-informed. I have followed the war closely, read news from various sources, watched the footage, and listened to interviews. My friends in Uzhgorod are people on the inside. Yes, I thought I was well-informed.

Now I sit in a restaurant, drinking wine, and listen to Oleg give his professional opinion on the different notes and flavours. He and his wife own a wine-importing business in Edinburgh.

'This is strange.'

'Why?' Oleg asks frowning.

'All this.' I spread my hands out and look around the restaurant.

'David. This is what people don't listen to. Maybe people get offended. I don't know. This is not my problem. They want a reality they understand. All of Ukraine. Big shit. But it is not a failed state and is not all the same. All of Ukraine is under an amber warning, but there are parts under red. These are the parts where no one is drinking water, never mind the wine.'

November 9th

ZHYTOMYR

We meet in the restaurant early the next morning with our backpacks. I lumber mine onto a chair and nearly tip it over. I'm a little tired, and my back is already starting to hurt from sitting in the car. Over breakfast, I swallow a couple of co-codamol tablets, purpose brought for the journey.

'Sore already?'

I laugh and nod.

'Well, at least you came prepared.'

To my surprise, I hear two men talking in English next to the buffet.

'That's a Yorkshire accent, I hear?' I say as a way of introduction.

'Leeds. That's me.'

'What are you doing over here?'

"Elping with police. That's me job back 'ome. 'ad to do something.'

Had to do something. No. He doesn't. But he is all the same.

'What's your name?'

'Sam.'

'David.'

'Nice to meet you, jock. Good luck.'

I'm reaching down for the sausages when the man Sam was speaking to before approaches me.

'Another British? My god,' he says when I nod. 'I'm Zorah.'

'David. Where are you from?'

'Israel. I worked with the dairy farmers here before the war. I'm trying to help people in Sumy. You know, they shot all the cows on two of the farms. Why? Why is this? I have seen some terrible things since I have been here. Some men only want an excuse to hold a gun, you know that? They don't care what it is. Then they get that gun, and they change.' He shakes his head sorrowfully. 'Where are you going?'

'Kharkiv Oblast.'

'Oh. Good luck. I mean it. Good luck.'

Finally, I get to see Zhytomyr. There is a park next to the hotel and a huge building opposite. Oleg reckons it's an administrative building. Whatever its function, the Ukrainian flag hanging from it is the biggest I have ever seen. It blocks the early morning sun and drapes half the pavement in shadow.

He goes to the car as I smoke. Another man smoking looks at me.

'Parlez vous Francais?'

'Non. Un petit peu,' I laugh.

'Ahhh, Britanski?'

'Oui.'

'Ahhh.' He points to himself. 'Georgian.'

'Tbilisi?'

'Yes! Yes!' He says, clearly delighted that I know where it is. 'Humanitarian?'

'Yes.'

'Ahhh, bon voyage. Bon voyage!' He smiles broadly and shakes my hand.

When we turn out of the hotel and back into the city, we both realise Zhytomyr is bigger than we thought. The roads are choked with rush hour traffic; the pavements are lined with pedestrians waiting on the bus or walking to work.

On the outskirts, half a dozen soldiers stand around a checkpoint, surrounded by sandbags and rustic blocks of concrete. They wave us through without checking our documents, and we rejoin the E40. We are, once more, surrounded by farmland for miles.

'The earth in Ukraine is incredibly fertile,' Oleg explains,' remember the patriots' flag? The black for the earth. Put anything into the Ukrainian ground, and it will grow.'

The drive to Kyiv is relatively short. Like much of our journey, we talk about the war. I probe him with questions. The conversation is gathering pace just as the car loses it. We hit a traffic jam a few kilometres from Kyiv. Checkpoints.

I have asked him about his thoughts on the aid given to Ukraine.

'Never underestimate the damage that can be done by acts of goodwill.' When he speaks, there is no hiding his frustration. 'I told you yesterday when I realised that sending food was wrong, it stopped. Clothes. I even realise now that the generator I have,' he jabs his thumb toward the back of the van,' we could get it here. There are many. Of course, Ukraine still needs support. The impression should not be that it doesn't. But the right kind of aid in the appropriate places. This is so important. As you said, we cannot make Ukraine weaker. Look at the traffic. The lorries. Meat for the restaurants? Products for the supermarket? Clothes? We keep sending free things; we are stopping people from living normal lives.'

We get stopped at the checkpoint and asked to pull over. Our passports are taken by a serious-looking soldier, who is considerably younger than either of us. He takes them into a small, camouflaged outpost. Inside, I can see a few more soldiers.

The soldier returns after a few minutes and hands us back the passports before waving us on.

'They know me.'

'Is that a good thing?'

'I don't know,' Oleg grins.

KYIV

09:32

It rose, all glass and skyscrapers, towering above us, like an Eastern European New York. Oleg corrects me on this, reminds me of the age difference. Yes, perhaps instead, New York is a Western version of Kyiv.

The Motherland Monument passes us. A huge statue that stands clutching a sword on top of Pechersk hill, the shed autumn leaves by its feet. Ukraine has been shedding herself for a long time now. Eight months of autumn. The monument stares out toward the North, the blade high and blazing in the sun. Surely this monument has never had a more fitting moment than now?

On either end of Paton Bridge, soldiers are installed, festooned against the stonework, their camouflage nets blowing in the Dnipro River breeze. They eye the passing traffic casually. Wartime or not, they know it would be unreasonable to stop traffic near the city centre during this hour. Not with the streets this jam-packed.

Pharmacies, supermarkets, gyms, and hotels. Here, I sense some of what Oleg has spoken about. The money. The opulence. The new apartments being advertised at prices that make my eyes water, even for someone native to Edinburgh. There is a bustle to the city. I crane my neck around to try and take it all in.

'War-torn city, eh?' Oleg remarks.

'It's unbelievable.'

'Better than many cities in Britain, I think.'

We pass through the city centre, although it is hard to tell where it ends and where it begins. Through a string of wide boulevards and now the Mother Monument is far behind, and we are surrounded by monoliths that are monuments of a different sort. Monuments to Ukraine's prosperity. The neon god flashes around us, and we are shoulder to shoulder in the traffic with expensive cars.

We trail the E40, which is stubbornly holding its course through all the mayhem, and eventually pop out the other side of the city. After a brief stop at another checkpoint, we are on the road to Kharkiv.

I doze off on the drive, and when I wake, it's time for lunch. We pull into a Wog and have a couple of burgers, some coffee, and a couple of cakes. I can see Oleg is tired. He has been driving for many days on his own. I go out for a smoke. A Porsche Tiagon pulls in to refuel. It is still refilling when Oleg comes out, and we go back to the van.

I can already see that he is tense. I initially put it down to fatigue, but as we pull onto the E40, he is shaking his head.

'What?'

'You see that back there?'

'What?'

'Porsche.'

'Yeah. Nice machine.'

'Yeah. Expensive machine. With the money made from selling this car, I could run Sunflower Scotland and feed many people in Kharkiv Oblast for months. This. This is not right.'

'In what way?'

'There are far wealthier people in Ukraine than us two. They give nothing. They could fill this van ten times. When I see these people, I honestly feel like they are laughing in my face. I'm the idiot who drives all the way from Scotland to help while they don't give a shit.'

'It is quite grotesque.'

'Yes. Grotesque. This is the word for it.'

'There is only what a person is willing to do and what they are not, Oleg.'

I admit, however, that I feel some of the annoyance Oleg does. We encounter many Nero's during our time in Ukraine, who fiddle while their country burns. Who won't give up their fancy lifestyles to support their country in an hour of need.

As we near Kharkiv, the traffic gets noticeably lighter. We pull into an Okko a few kilometres outside of the city. Here we meet Daniel. His Mitsubishi four-by-four is tattooed with Sunflower Scotland stickers.

He approaches the car, and Oleg jumps out. They embrace more like a father and son than colleagues in a charity. Daniel goes back to his car and brings us a cake and some flowers. He welcomes me in English, and we shake hands. They chat for a time, and then Oleg gets back in the car.

'Can I go with Daniel?'

'Yes. Of course.'

Ever since I was introduced to the work Sunflower Scotland was doing in Ukraine, I had heard about this semi-mythical person.

He explains some of what he has done in broken English and uses a translator when he struggles to articulate his thoughts. He has been delivering food packages to frontline villages and towns for much of the war. He turned twenty a couple of weeks before we arrived.

We are stopped for a few minutes at the checkpoint outside of the city. He leaves the car with a couple of soldiers.

'A minute,' he says.

When he returns, he says, 'where we are going, they check harder.'

KHARKIV

16:33

We continue to talk on google translate as we make our way into another city shrouded in darkness. Like Zhytomyr, the streetlights are off. But even at that disadvantage, I can tell Kharkiv is a far bigger city. Ukraine's second city. Over three times bigger than Edinburgh.

He explains that he used to work for a Ukrainian-based charity before Sunflower. He gives a dry smile when he describes going to frontline villages and towns in his Orange Sedan, six hundred thousand miles on the clock. Less than ideal for the roads he was travelling. He had no bulletproof vest. No helmet. All these things have been remedied since he joined Sunflower. He taps the dashboard at a red light.

'Good car. I am very happy with this car. How was the travelling? Are you tired?'

'Yes. But positive. Happy to be here.'

'Oleg is tired?'

'Yes. Lots of driving. But he is good.'

'Good.'

Despite his youthfulness, there are bags under his eyes. I ask him if he is tired.

'Yes. I have been off for ten days.'

'Why are you tired then?' I ask, and we laugh.

'Kozacha Lopan. Heavy departure.'

One of his last food parcel drop-offs was in this village. He was shelled whilst there. Not the first time. But it shook him up. He has taken time away from the frontline since to recover.

Then I see, for the first time, a physical sign of the war. A tenement block that has been destroyed, a gaping void, with the floors exposed. On the top level, I see a bathtub.

'Russian fascists,' Daniel says.

After a period of silence, Daniel talks into his phone and repeats the translation back in English.

'Many of my schoolmates have died,' he reels off the names. Out of respect to the families, we decided not to include these names in the text. But there are many. 'Two girls in steelworks of Mariupol.'

'Christ. Were they fighting?'

'Some were fighting. Some just bombs.'

Just bombs. Daniel says it in a matter-of-fact tone, as if he is talking about the weather. Some days it rains. Some days it doesn't. Some days my old schoolmates are killed by bombs. We pass another few wrecked buildings. These are not intentionally singled out by Daniel; they are simply on the route to the warehouse where we are going to unpack the van. A fog has descended, and now these broken buildings leer out, near invisible until the moment we pass them, only visible in the headlights, like ghostly apparitions of the city that used to be.

It's pitch black. Our warehouse is more of a garage, and there are hundreds of these units grouped together. A man calls out through the night and raises the bar to let us enter the compound. When Daniel kills the lights of the Mitsubishi, he pulls out a flashlight from the inside of his door. Once he's finished opening it up, we set down a few torches and light the garage as best we can. We unpack the thermals but leave the aid we have for the hospital we are to visit tomorrow. The food will be purchased over the next couple of days. The bags wait to be filled in the corner. I look at the silver emblem on the black and struggle to read it in the half-light.

'Russian warship. Go fuck yourself,' Oleg says with a grin. It's become an immortalized saying of the war. A statement of resilience that seems to have echoed across the whole of

Ukraine ever since it was uttered by Ukrainian soldiers in defiance of the Russian army's order to surrender at Snake Island. Daniel smirks and repeats it in Ukrainian.

We head back into the city to check in to the hotel. The curfew in Kharkiv is earlier than Zhytomyr. 9 pm. Sharp. It ends at 6 am.

Oleg has stayed at the hotel before, on his previous trip in August. He hopes it lasts better than his previous accommodation did in July, which was hit by a shell a few days after his departure. Like Zhytomyr, it is lovely. The room is excellent. I find myself lulled into a state of false security. It is already nearly 7.30 pm. But in those few minutes in the room, while I drop off my stuff and have a quick wash before we go to dinner, I think again about where I am.

I am kitted out with an array of electrical goods in preparation for hardship. A powerful lantern, two power banks, over forty batteries, and other utilities. But the room is warm and quite lovely. No problem with electricity.

We round the corner to a place where Oleg dines when he is staying at the hotel. I am acutely aware of the curfew time, as anyone is that has not been under the constraint before. But the restaurant staff greet us cheerily and give us a seat in the window. The restaurant is nearly full. Ottantotto 88. A great

Italian restaurant. If you ever visit Kharkiv, I strongly recommend it. We dined here every night during our stay.

We have borsht, salads, and beers. When the plates are cleared, Oleg gets a few things out of his bag. Caramel wafers and miniature bottles of whisky. Even some haggis and a few other Scottish mementoes. It's Daniel's belated birthday present. Daniel smiles broadly at this, and they share another hug.

Daniel leaves us not long after; he still has to drive home before the curfew comes into effect. Oleg and I make the short walk back to the hotel.

After a cup of tea and a bit of the cake Daniel has given us, we go to our rooms. I stare out of the window when I get there; the street is nothing more than a dark void.

November 10th

KHARKIV

'Bo bach! Bo bach! Means rocket,' Daniel explains when I look at his cracked phone. It was broken from when he went to ground under shellfire in Kupiansk. 'Bach. Bach. Shelling.'

We share in this light-hearted chat while stuck in the morning traffic. This traffic, however, is not caused by the checkpoints. Daniel smiles and leans back. I don't think I've ever seen someone so happy to be stuck in a traffic jam. The people have come back, he tells me. It's a good sign.

Only the night before, I had a conversation with the receptionist Julia. Thanks to the wonderful planning of Oleg, there is a little private area at the back of the hotel reserved for people like me. She joined me after I had finished my cigarette, and I chain-smoked another two while she told me about some of her experiences.

She had fled Kharkiv at the start of the war with her parents. Then the village they had fled to came under attack. Her parents had been on the balcony when the artillery had started firing. They ran inside just in time, and although they got many cuts from the glass which shattered behind them, it could have been a lot worse. They survived. The people that had lived above them on the twelfth floor hadn't been so lucky. The entire level was destroyed.

Daniel doesn't remain happy for too long. There are too many scars in his city. Too many reminders. We pass one particularly large apartment building, with scorch marks around the window frames long void of glass.

'Many people died,' he says. 'Civilians. Civilians. Civilians. No military.'

The fog has not dissipated from the night before. As we take the road out of the East of Kharkiv, the headlights of cars move like silver orbs through the mist. A team of soldiers is on the strip of land that separates either side of the motorway. Daniel tells me that they are sweeping for mines—just a precaution.

We stop at the side of the road. Oleg hops out of his car, and Daniel asks me to accompany him. There is a huge sign at the side of the road. Chuhuiv.

'This was a very dangerous place,' Oleg tells me, 'bombs used to drop daily.'

On his previous mission in July, they had taken the same road to deliver aid to Chuhuiv. A few days later, it was heavily shelled. Only two months previous, the road that we drive on was cratered and potholed. It has since been completely repaired and resurfaced

This part of the war effort can be easily overlooked. The fighting on the front and the seemingly endless stream of death understandably takes up much of the spotlight. But the rebuilding of infrastructure and the reliability of the workmen who keep Ukraine going should never be undervalued. Indeed, the reaction time of the Ukrainians to repair the damage is astonishing. Surely this is almost as important as the fighting itself. The Russians expended so much effort, so many resources, manpower, and weaponry, and now only a couple of months later, there is little to show for it.

CHUHUIV
09:36

The hospital we are going to was hit three weeks ago. A large crater marks the ground in front of the building. Dozens of windows are boarded up. Fortunately, the damage was largely superficial. Twenty yards in the wrong direction, and it could have been far worse. The Caduceus insignia is high up the wall, the two serpents twisting around, a chunk of concrete missing from the tip of one of their tails.

The importance of the Chuhuiv hospital grew after Kupiansk and Balakliya fell to the Russians. Many patients were redirected here, and on his last visit, Daniel said the maternity ward was full to the brim. Babies born under bombs.

Welcome to planet Earth little ones. I have a young son back in Edinburgh. I cannot imagine what it is like to bring a child into this world under these circumstances.

I begin to unload a couple of wheelchairs while Daniel and Oleg speak to the doctor and deal with the paperwork. Then the three of us unload the adult pads, the crutches, and the walk assisters. The doctor, a fatigued man whose skin looks grey with exhaustion, shakes our hands without a smile and thanks us before disappearing into a ward.

We make our way around the building, stepping around the crater with the mum's bags. The bags are filled with essentials that new mothers might need. To Oleg's irritation, we realise after a couple of days in Kharkiv that even these specific products could have been bought in Ukraine. This is another indicator of the rapidity with which the face of the war can change. A month and a half ago, it would have been unthinkable to have got some of these specialised products in Kharkiv. Now, they are back in abundance. It frustrates Oleg but is another lesson learned and another alteration to be made.

Daniel looks surprised. When we arrive at the maternity ward, he looks down the corridor. At first, I think he is looking for doctors or nurses. He says something to Oleg, who turns to me and translates.

'It's totally different from his last visit. Far quieter.'

A small blonde nurse approaches us; she is smiling. 'Dobre Ranok,' she says pleasantly. We pass her a couple of the bags, and the three of them chat in Ukrainian for a time. I study the pictures of the newborns pinned to the noticeboard. Small handwritten notes and drawings of hearts are tacked up next to them.

It only takes one more visit to drop off enough bags for the new mothers in the maternity ward. We are leaving far fewer bags than we had planned.

'There it is,' Oleg says when we leave the hospital, 'less babies. Kupiansk and Balakliya have been liberated, so released some of the pressure on here, but this was not the main reason we haven't seen as many babies. A lot of men are fighting, and people do not want to get pregnant during wartime. So, there it is. We are literally seeing a gap in the fabric of life itself.'

MALA ROHAN

11:52

We take a break from those lovely smooth Ukrainian roads on the way back to Kharkiv and turn off onto a dirt road. I have no idea at this moment where we are going. I think we are going somewhere to gather supplies, perhaps to buy the food for the packages.

We idle at a slow speed, Daniel twisting and turning the steering wheel, like some wild sea captain in a storm, desperately trying to avoid the worst potholes. Oleg calls from the van, and after a brief conversation, Daniel brings the Mitsubishi to a halt, and Oleg joins us.

Either side of us, we are surrounded by the meadow. The wildflowers have lost their colour. The grasses are turning yellow. There is a chill in the air.

Looking down the road, I can see it doesn't improve, but I'm beckoned back with a 'davai. Davai,' by Daniel, and we carry on regardless. The road becomes shaded in tree cover, and then two burnt-out buildings appear, flanking either side of us.

'This area Russian. Russian quarters,' Daniel says, pointing at the buildings. Destroyed buildings are scattered around us now.

'Russian world,' says Daniel.

We drive on in silence for some time, taking another small road that leads down the hill.

VILKHIVKA

12:26

We drive over a short bridge at the bottom of the hill and ascend on the other side. On the crest above us, a small village appears. Vilkhivka.

We stop the cars in the middle of the village and get out. Destroyed homes, craters and the scorch marks of shelling surround us. I take a few steps from the car, but Daniel reaches for me and gently takes my arm. He points at the grass.

'No walk. Stay on asphalt,' Daniel says. He explains that if the ground was soft when the bombardment happened, then there might be unexploded bombs still in the ground. He looks around and declares something a lot more obvious. 'Many died.'

I pick up three spent bullet cartridges. One of the windows in the house nearest has bullet holes, and the surrounding walls are scattered with the pinpricks of gunfire.

'So this is the face of Putin's liberation, eh? Strange liberation,' Oleg says as he passes me.

The house next door has a mangled couch sticking out of a gaping hole. The brickwork is strewn through the garden. A TV sits in the corner, the exposed timbers of the roof next to it, blackened and charred, windows blown out from the inside. All around is the same and yet different. I did not know there were so many ways to destroy a home. Some had their walls blown away. Others their roofs. Some were reduced to their very foundations. But the whole place does have one thing which unifies it. It gives the eerie feeling that we are following in the footsteps of death.

I walk down the road. Melted soles from a pair of shoes. A broken pedal from a bike. And on the ground, black marks where cars exploded. They cling there like burnt shadows.

Daniel points at a long rectangular burn on the road. 'This was a bus. It was full of people.'

Then I see an anomaly. A house that is intact and a man outside that house, busying away in the garden. A small glimpse, perhaps, of what life had been like in the village before most of it had been turned to rubble. I briefly consider going to chat with him, but my appetite for conversation is gone.

Oleg and Daniel talk quietly for a couple of minutes. Oleg turns to me. 'This was done in May. It was not when the Russians were advancing but when they were retreating.'

'Bo bach,' Daniel says.

'Bo back,' I echo.

'Fuck Putin.'

'Fuck Putin.'

The area around the village has seen heavy fighting. We see the signs as we drive along the road. Many of the residential buildings that pepper the landscape are now empty shells. No soul could live in them, even if they wanted to. But it is nowhere near the same scale. Vilkhivka is all misery and destruction.

We come to a checkpoint a couple of kilometres away from Vikhivka. This checkpoint is the most fortified I have seen so far. Trenches are dug, and a minefield has been laid a little way behind. It was put down to halt the Russian advance.

Daniel curses under his breath a few times as we pass a destroyed three-storey residential building. Every couple of kilometres, there are reminders.

'Do you ever think Russia and Ukraine will have a relationship like they did before?'

'There is no possibilities for friendship. They violate the,' he pauses for a second and speaks into his phone,' sovereignty of our country in 2014, and all friendship has vanished since. I think there should be a one-mile-high fence between our two countries, and we shouldn't see each other in this world.'

KHARKIV

17:03

We are sifting quickly through the boxes of thermals, dividing them into half. Three hundred thermals, divvied into different sizes. Medium. Large. Extra large. Extra extra large. Oleg has marked the boxes in Ukrainian for the army brigade and squadron we are meeting. A last-minute change of plans means one of them is coming to Kharkiv tonight to collect. In the darkness, we rummage about, my lantern and the torches doing their best but still inadequate. We curse and sweat for an hour, labouring to get it ready for the commander coming to meet us.

Five minutes after we finish filling the last box, headlights swing into the compound. I have not written the name of the commander, or the two young soldiers who accompanied him, or even the name of the Brigade out of respect to the situation. This is an information war, and it's imperative that some details are left out.

The commander gives us all a strong handshake while the two soldiers busy themselves filling their van. Oleg disappears into the garage for a moment and comes out, heaving a generator. The two young men take it off him. They speak in Ukrainian for some time. I find out later that they are discussing the front, which I wouldn't have guessed from the way they are speaking. I tap my cigarette packet towards the commander, and he takes one from me.

'Dyakuyu,' he says and smiles.

Oleg translates parts of the conversation. The atmosphere is easy, there is much laughter, and they remain for nearly half an hour talking. The young soldiers contribute; one accepts a cigarette from me, and the other doesn't smoke. An unusual thing in Ukraine. They talk freely, and despite their youthful years, like Daniel, they are already men. It strikes me how old these young people are. They belong. They are confident of their place.

By the time they leave, the night has drawn close, and the cold is starting to get in our bones. Daniel doesn't join us for dinner, so only Oleg and I are at the restaurant. We order the Borscht and some pasta. I order the Ketel, a massively underrated vodka. Here the standard pour is fifty millilitres. It soon warms me up.

Oleg asks me what I thought of the day. He's interested to know my take. He talks of how being exposed to the war has changed him and his reaction to places like Vilkhivka. He still remembers the first time he saw it.

I take some time answering him. I am not sure the things I have seen that day can ever really be processed, if the sight of war is able to be explained.

'Today. I saw the other face of humanity. I had seen it in pictures before and seen the words written down, but here to see it…in the flesh.' I shake my head, and I can feel tears coming to my eyes. 'It is hard to see. It's not a news story. It's not on TV or online. It's there right in front of you. Murder.'

I sling the remainder of the vodka down my throat. 'What a species.'

A common word used by the Ukrainian army for Russian soldiers, and it was used by one of the young soldiers that we met this evening at the garage, is Orks. This is not meant merely as a flippant term of disrespect or a sign of disgust at what has happened. It is an admission that it is hard to believe that humans can do such things. They have ceased to be men and have become monsters. Orks.

'Why didn't they leave?' I ask.

'I don't know if they had a chance in Vilkhivka. But even if they did, the first hurdle many Ukrainians, especially in rural areas, must overcome is a lack of money. Many British have savings, not so the case with Ukrainians.

They get offered pitiful financial support by the government to relocate. A lot of Ukrainians simply cannot afford to leave their village, towns, and cities.'

We are halfway through our dinner before another question, one that I have been meaning to ask ever since we crossed the border, comes to mind.

'Where are the bomb shelters?'

'I can show you.'

'You use them?'

'No. Not many do. Daniel never would.'

'Why?'

'If the shelling is near you, you can be very easily buried alive. The first time I came to Kharkiv, I thought about it. The bombing was severe. I followed the two-wall rule. This is when you leave a room that is nearest to the street and go to the corridor or something. Two walls between you and outside. No. I will never use a bomb shelter.

It's luck if you survive, I think. Some die. Some live. It's luck.'

I thought of the lone villager back in Vilkhivka—Russian roulette on an international scale.

November 11th

The first stop of the day is another maternity hospital. This one is in Kharkiv itself. We arrive fifteen minutes late, and the mothers are already waiting outside with their strollers and bassinets. As soon as I catch sight of Oleg getting out of the other car, I can see he's not happy. But we're committed. We're here.

We hand out the bags, take a few pictures as evidence of where the aid is going, and move on. It's all over in five minutes. As always, the people running the maternity ward and the new mothers show their appreciation, but I can sense why Oleg has some trepidation about the drop-off. My suspicions are confirmed when we stop to get fuel and have a coffee at the gas station.

'I'm very disappointed. This is not what we are about. We're not in the business of giving aid to mothers with apple watches.'

I'm learning that this is the way of things. Even with Daniel and Oleg's combined knowledge and good intentions, mistakes happen. So, imagine trying to achieve anything without either.

Oleg flinches, almost like a spasm he stretches out his hand. 'What am I talking about. I am so ashamed. What am I talking about.' Periodically, Oleg has these moments of self-flagellation. 'These women were pregnant and may have even given birth during the bombardment—my God. Things are changing so fast. But there is something good here. Something good,' he nods. 'It shows real life is coming back to Kharkiv. It shows it is recovering,' he concludes.

We stop at a shopping mall to collect supplies for our next trip out. From the outside, my expectations are low, but they are confounded the moment we walk through the front doors. The mall itself is split between two floors. On the ground floor is a huge supermarket. Oleg and I go in together. I think some of the locals must believe we are a bit strange, photographing as we go, but the selection of produce is astounding. The fish section beats anything I have seen in a Scottish supermarket. The cheese section takes up twice the space of my local upmarket shop. The bakery is massive and offers a huge variety of baked goods.

We pick up what we need, but Oleg says we should see the second floor before we leave. A hardware shop, a pharmacist, a shop that specialises in ceramics, and a café with an inviting-looking menu. The whole place, bottom and top floor is bustling with shoppers.

Oleg disappears into one of the shops, and when he reappears, he hands me a small notebook with "Ukraine" and the country's emblem etched onto the front cover. Much of what I write here was written in it. It reminds me of what Oleg has repeatedly said whenever I look at it and think of that mall. Ukraine is not a failed state.

We arrive at the wholesalers to purchase the food we will be putting into the food packages around mid-morning. The bags are to be filled today.

The wholesalers consists of dozens of shops and enormous warehouses. When we enter, it reminds me of a Moroccan souk. Narrow roads, barely wide enough to fit two cars coming in opposite directions, wind their way past the paint-chipped shopfronts. Cars are parked where they can fit, and people are milling around the doorways, carrying sacks of produce and cases of oil and water. We have to wait patiently as a huge lorry makes its way out from near one of the warehouses and grumbles its way through the throng. It's a controlled mayhem, like any such place always is, a hive of activity. There must be at least a thousand people moving in and out of the doorways and crowding the aisles, the shelves choked full of goods. Hastily handwritten tags are stuck beneath each item to show the price. In short, if you are claustrophobic, this is the last place you would want to visit on the planet.

I am slightly relieved when we deviate away, far from the madding crowd, and turn a corner next to one of the behemoth warehouses. We park and a man comes out. He is smiling and welcomes Daniel with a handshake.

The warehouse is like an enlarged version of one of the shops. It, too, is stocked from floor to ceiling, but instead of loose cans and packets, there are whole pallets. They rest on wielded metal shelves, the heavy-duty kind that look like they could bear the weight of a resting elephant.

Oleg has some paperwork, and after a friendly chat with the proprietor, we begin to load the van. I am not sure what I was expecting, and perhaps, in hindsight, this does me a favour. Seven pallets. We form a human chain and unload the pasta, tomato sauce, condensed milk, tea, barley, sugar, salt, oats, and toilet paper into the van and Daniel's car.

There isn't nearly enough space to do it all in one trip. We drive back to the garage, build another human chain, unload, and return for the second lot. Only through creative filling of the van and car do we narrowly avoid the need for a third trip.

We unload, and despite the November chill, we are all perspiring by the time we are finished. We take a short break. We drink the sweet tea Daniel's mum prepared for us and eat some chocolate.

Daniel has been doing this work for months. Sometimes his mum comes and helps him. Sometimes his girlfriend too.

But often, he is left to do it alone. By the end of the day, I have even more respect for him.

He explains how it is done efficiently, and we get to work. In the contents of each bag, there are three bags of pasta, three bags of barley, sugar, condensed milk, tomato paste, salt, oats, sausages, and toilet paper. Enough to feed a couple of people for a week to ten days.

My job is to fill the bags with pasta, tomato paste, salt, and toilet paper. Oleg and Daniel divvy the other items up between them, and we work steadily for the next few hours, filling ten bags at a time.

By the end, there is a small mountain of bags behind us.

"Russian warship. Go fuck yourself."

As well as the food packages, we are also delivering the rest of the thermals and a couple of camouflage nets to a unit down at Izium. Once we've finished packing the van and Daniel's car, we have another cup of tea. Oleg turns to me.

'Tomorrow, we go to Borova.'

When we met the soldiers the previous evening, Oleg and Daniel asked them about specific villages in the frontline that we can stop at on the way to Izium. The soldiers tell them not to go to the first village they had planned, as very few people have remained. Oleg and Daniel's backup option is Borova, a village just across the Oskil River, fifteen kilometres from the front. The soldiers confirm that the town needs aid, but they warn us that the road is dangerous. It is heavily mined.

After discussing the mines, the three of us are silent for some time. Oleg has his phone out and beckons me over. He shows me pictures of the mines.

They aren't at all what I expected. They are small, barely longer than my lighter. They resemble brown and green butterflies. I think of my little boy back in Edinburgh—his fascination with insects and animals. I imagine him rummaging about in the undergrowth, as he frequently does. It is all I can do to stop thinking about it.

Oleg explains that they won't kill but are enough to blow off a foot.

There are larger mines as well, but the little butterflies are the ones the Russians used most liberally in the area.

'No wandering from the cars,' he says.

A week after we return to Edinburgh, two volunteers were killed on this road by landmines. I saw the pictures; their humanitarian aid exploded across the road. Loaves of bread burrowed into the surrounding bushes.

They knew the risk, as we did. Like us, they were simply trying to do the right thing. I feel a remarkable sorrow for these complete strangers. May they rest in peace.

Daniel is busy locking up when Oleg has an outburst. He cheers for a moment, his eyes glued to the screen of his phone.

'Kherson has been liberated.'

Daniel comes out of the door, and Oleg calls over to him. It's quite an emotional moment. We share many hugs and handshakes. But there are no tears. Indeed, I sense a stoicism in Daniel. Tears can come later. The war is not over yet. But the momentum has turned. It has been turning for two months now. There is a real belief in Ukrainians and Daniel that the war is only going one way.

But it's not over yet.

November 12th

There is a frost. The temperatures dropped the night before. I had to unstick the ashtray from the wall at the back of the hotel when I went for my cigarette. Through thermals and two layers, I can feel the cold. I make myself a quadruple-shot coffee and sit down in the foyer. Oleg comes down a couple of minutes later. He goes to the car and brings it around the front of the hotel. By the time I am finished with my coffee, he already has his body armour and helmet on.

Daniel pulls up. He is suited and booted too. He takes my body armour and helmet off the back seat and helps me get it on. It weighs me down, and the helmet feels awkward. He smiles reassuringly.

'Strange first time, yes?'

I grin back. 'Yes.'

He helps me stick the patches onto the velcro: my name and a British flag. Oleg comes over.

'So you can be identified,' he says with a laugh and slaps me on the shoulder.

We drive through the streets of Kharkiv, smoking out of the windows and listening to "Kampfire Vampire" by Gerry Cinnamon. Daniel wanted to hear a Scottish artist. In return, he plays me some Ukrainian artists. Skofka, "we won't forget, and we won't forgive."

The war and defiant national pride. There has been a massive wave of music inspired by these themes since the invasion. Art can tell you a lot about the heart of a country. The message is clear. Ukrainians are united. Ukrainians stand together.

It doesn't really matter where you drive through Kharkiv; no route makes the marks of the war invisible. Tenement blocks. Businesses. Hotels. Civilians, as Daniel says.

Daniel takes my attention away from what is on the other side of the windscreen by tugging at the collar of his jacket.

'Yeah, nice jacket.'

And it is—a proper winter jacket.

'I won it in a competition,' Daniel explains.

'What competition?'

'Errrr….' He pauses, searching for the word. 'Sumo.'

'In Sumy?'

He looks slightly puzzled. He gets his phone and speaks into it, repeats back the translation. 'I won it in a sumo competition.'

'Fuck off!'

Daniel bursts out laughing. I look at this nimble wee boy and can't imagine it. He is slender, even with the additional body armour. Fortunately, he has proof, otherwise, I might never have believed him. His mother's Instagram. Daniel appears on the screen inside a sumo ring, dressed in traditional attire and fighting.

'Fuck off!'

We both laugh just as we leave the suburbs of Kharkiv behind us; the early fog is just beginning to disperse.

We don't have to drive far from Kharkiv to see the damage of the war. After the first checkpoint, roughly fifteen minutes away from the city, we pass the burnt-out carcass of a car at the side of the road. Daniel points at it.

'Volunteers.'

'Shell?'

'Yes.'

The farther we drive, the more we see. However, it's not all doom and gloom. The wreck of a Russian tank passes us, deserted in the middle of a field.

'We fuck Putin.'

At a checkpoint outside Shevchenko, a soldier wishes us good luck in English. It is a village that has been occupied. The soldier is jolly. He salutes us off, and I see him grin in the wing mirrors.

A little way down the road, we stop. Oleg has called and wants a picture with Daniel next to a sign. A sign that only two months previous was well out of reach. He hops out, and together, the three of us cross the road. We walk along the fringes of it but never off it. I feel skittish imagining what surprises might be lurking in the grass. I am reassured that this part is not mined.

The rusted sign points the way to Kupiansk airport. Oleg and Daniel pose. I light up, and the mood is easy. Jovial, as it has been for all the trip so far. Then, the sound of artillery. Daniel speaks quickly to Oleg.

'It's Russian. In the car. Let's go,' Oleg says, his back already to me. I have to jog to catch up with Daniel.

I have seen the destruction. Now I have heard it for the first time—thunderclaps and then silence.

KUPIANSK

09:15

Hundreds of Ukrainian flags flutter in the wind. Flags are attached to any surface that the locals think will be able to bare the weight. At first, we see nothing. The dashboard rattles as we ride over the uneven road. The roads are getting worse.

A man passes us on a motorbike. We slow to let an old man cross the road. Then, as we descend the slope further into the town, the buildings appear.

First, a factory. Its huge roof has been obliterated, parts of the substructure poke out toward the road, the interior gouged out by the shelling. Wiring hangs loose. The rubble has spilled across the walkway and part of the road. Then another factory. This one has all the walls removed, but the metal infrastructure underneath has retained its shape. It stands as a skeleton. The metal bones look like they could collapse at any time, burnished dark orange by the flames that have engulfed them, the last surviving parts of the cremation.

Two blocks of residential housing with all the windows blown out, the burns marks around the window frames. As we exit the town on the East side, a desecrated group of houses pass us. We rumble up the road.

'Russian fascists,' Daniel says quietly.

KUPIANSK-VUZLOVYI

09:23

'Oh fuck. Fuck,' Daniel says.

He stabs at the brakes until we nearly halt. We are at the top of a road staring down into a valley. The Oskil river runs in the background. But neither of us care about that. We are both staring at the same thing. What else could we stare at?

I saw not one building standing.

'Civilians,' Daniel says. I can see he is as emotionally shocked as I am.

Not even the trees along the riverbank have been spared. Their branches are touching the river, bobbing up and down in the current, most of them with their trunks broken off around the middle. Splinters are scattered on the ground and mingle with the ones from the houses. In Kupiansk, at least we could decipher what type of buildings had been destroyed. Here, not even that is possible. The settlement has been wiped from the face of the earth. The surrounding hillside is so heavily cratered that it looks as if it belongs to another planet.

A small temporary bridge has been erected across the river. It is wide enough, just, and has an intimidating ten-inch gap running down the middle of it. Daniel doesn't flinch. We ease across the Oskil and leave the devastated settlement behind.

KURYLIVSKA

09:34

I watch the cars ahead bob up and down on the road and feel our own rock and shake. From afar, we must look like a desperate convoy. A big building to our left passes. Another factory of some sort destroyed. Then a building that appears to have something to do with infrastructure. Electricity perhaps. It's hard to tell. Of course, there are more shelled-out houses. Of course. *Just bombs.*

A pair of old women wait on us to pass at the street corner. They watch us closely as we pass. They watch us as if to say, "what kind of mad fool would be here by choice?"

Oleg calls, and we stop in the town. They discuss directions and then we get back in the cars. A ruined church and, next to it, a building with soldiers around it. It looks as though they are moving aid.

The road out of town is rutted. We spot another wrecked Russian tank, this one on its side in a ditch at the side of the road. The undercarriage is exposed to us, torn right through. When I stare at it, I can see the sky on the other side.

Then a final block of apartments appears, and we can do the same thing with them. Ripped through, from side to side. Massive parts have collapsed. Staring at the front of them, nothing but a cloud in the distance behind.

On the opposite side of the road, a field of dead unharvested sunflowers, black as the soil.

The rutted road never seems to end. As we enter a village, I raise my camera to film. Daniel grabs my arm and nods out the window. Not a stone's throw away, a tank that is not wrecked. A Ukrainian tank. It is camouflaged in the trees. If Daniel had not pointed it out, then I might never have seen it. Then I see more and more. Vehicles of different types, some simple troop transports, and jeeps, others more sinister looking.

'They see you, they take phone, and then,' he clenches his fist and punches his open palm.

'Ok.'

Due to the high concentration of military, these villages shall remain nameless.

Between the villages stretches meadows and farmland. Flat. Very flat. It is quite beautiful. Now we rock with the rhythm of the car, and I get a sense of peace. An odd thing to feel in a warzone, perhaps. But it is a peaceful place—all those meadows and farmland. Here I film. It is quite beautiful. I turn the camera to Daniel and tell him to smile. He grins at me and then points out of his window.

'Three kilometre. Frontline. We are very close.'

A few minutes later, we are halted by a Ukrainian soldier. He lifts his hand but offers no explanation. Behind him, a car is parked across the road to stop anyone from trying to pass. Then we hear artillery fire.

'Russian or Ukrainian?'

'Not sure,' Daniel replies.

A couple of explosions erupt in the field to our left. They are quite far away. Then we hear machine gun fire. It's the Ukrainians testing the equipment. The soldier who barred our way gets into the stationary car blocking the road and pulls off onto the side. He sticks his hand out of the window and casually waves us through. We pass two dozen Ukrainian soldiers. One lets off another volley from the machine gun just as we pass.

BOROVA

11:28

Borova was only liberated in the September offensive. It had been under Russian occupation for a considerable amount of time. Out of the villages and towns we have been through so far, it has actually faired better in terms of physical damage. But what can be seen isn't all that matters. Things can be hidden. You cannot always see in a stare whether someone is unemployed. Whether they have lost loved ones. Whether their home is destroyed. Whether they haven't eaten in two days.

We initially drive through the town, looking for the best place to stop off and give out the food packages. The square we pass might do. But there is a crater, and the glass has been smashed out of the building next to it. We see no better alternatives and double back. It's clear that this is not Oleg or

Daniel's first time. They both call out their windows to a couple of passers-by, and by the time we are all out of the vehicles, the first three or four people are making their way towards us.

From the sports cars of Kyiv to the bikes of Borova. Dull grey and rusted, they look soviet made and squeak toward us, the riders swinging from side to side, trying to keep them in a straight line. The old and the young come, and soon there are bikes lying on their sides all around us.

One hundred and twenty bags gone in fifteen minutes. That's one bag given away every eight seconds. When we get down to the last few bags, things become less peaceful. There is a hint of desperation.

A couple of older women get thrust forward from the back of the semi-functioning queue. I can see the drawn faces on some of the men that have pushed them forward. They look like they need the food packages just as much.

When the last bag is taken, and there is no more, one or two people show their discontent. Daniel speaks with a tone I'm not familiar with him using, and the heckles die down. Now, more than ever, I wish I could communicate with them. Do they not understand? If we could bring enough food for everyone, we would.

THE ROAD TO IZIUM
RUBTSI
12:35

The road becomes worse. We trundle along it, swerving from side to side. Rules of the road no longer apply. Besides, we see no other cars for half hour stretches.

By now, Daniel has already been driving for the best part of six hours, and despite his commendable stamina, even he admits he is getting tired.

Rubtsi appears up ahead. It is shell smashed and largely annihilated. I am still stunned by the scale of destruction, but already I have an uneasy sense of getting numb to it. Another cracked house. Another destroyed factory. *Just bombs.*

Then we pass a destroyed nursery. Chunks of brick and plaster lie among the swings, shoots, and other playground paraphernalia, all of which remain oddly untouched as if they are simply waiting for the children to return and use them. A little shelter with colourful drawings on it, something for the children to hide under when it rains, is split down the middle. Half of a women's smile is missing.

YATSKIVKA

12:42

The vine is fat with fruit. The branches are bent under the weight. They rest on the top of the fence. Behind, a house that looks like it was once lovely. Now, it is derelict. The fence may be the only salvageable thing on the entire plot. The grapes are engorged.

Yatskivka is a little town in a forest. It sits on the border between Kharkiv Oblast and Donetsk Oblast. It's clear from the top of the hill, looking down at the town, that Yatskivka is going to need a lot of rebuilding to be anything like the town it once was.

The first thing we see when we enter is the church steeple. The roof around it is burnt away, yet somehow the steeple remains. The pews are empty and wetted by the early morning dew. The congregation is long gone. As with all these villages and towns, I wonder where the people have gone. Many will have died, but those that escaped, homeless and destitute, where did they go? Where do they end up?

When we stop next to the sign that marks the border between the two Oblasts, I approach Oleg. All three of us are silent. Next to us is an electric substation. The fence twisted by a shell strike, the utility system open with strands of wire and other parts of machinery sprung out like a jack-in-the-box. Very little is said between the three of us.

The engineers are working diligently. I can hear them shouting to each other above the noise of the industrial machines: the diggers and the small crane. The bridge is shattered in the middle. Shelling or by planted explosives, it's impossible to tell. We wait in the queue to use the pontoon bridge. The car making the crossing ahead of us is a Lada. An old Soviet-era car. It's hard to believe it's capable of driving on the roads we've just been down. It splashes off the far end of the pontoon and rides through the shallows of the Oskil river on the far side.

'Shit,' Daniel says.

When it comes to our turn, Daniel puts the four to four to good use and crashes through the shale and water; the waves come up high on our windows. He accelerates the car up the hill toward the checkpoint, pausing briefly to ensure that Oleg has no problems negotiating the not-quite-big enough pontoon.

Here the military presence is strong again. The checkpoints more fortified. The soldiers retain their upbeat demeanours but appear much more serious. Their stares last a little longer. The passports are checked just a little more thoroughly. This has been the scene of intense fighting.

IZIUM

13:14

When I discovered we would be going to Izium, I was quite shocked. Like many who have followed the war closely, the name Izium has become synonymous with the brutality of the invasion. In only one of the mass graves found on the outskirts of the city, at least four hundred and forty bodies were uncovered. To date, twenty-two of the people found in this mass grave were military. The rest are believed to be civilians. Five children have been found.

The train station is desolate. Sheets of metal, as long as football pitches are bent and twisted, and lumber on the side of the metal girders. They must weigh a tonne, maybe more, yet the way they rest, it looks like a breeze could bring them down. We only travel into the beginnings of the town. Daniel gets a call. It's from the commander we've arranged to meet. We turn around and head back to the city limits, where a sign carrying the town's name sits twenty feet tall.

After a few minutes of waiting, a man pulls up in a white van behind us. He greets us effusively. Multiple handshakes are shared, he shakes my hand three times alone, and we slap each other on the back. For purposes of military security, I will call him Yuri. The warmth of Yuri is clear right away. There is a smile always dancing in his eyes, and he speaks quickly and with enthusiasm.

'Dyakuyu! Dyakuyu!' He gushes when we give him the boxes of thermals. Then we put the camouflage nets and sleeping bags into the back of his van. After a few photos together, he speaks with Oleg and Daniel, and we get back in our vehicles. We reach the checkpoint we came in on, but instead of sticking to the main road, we pull off onto a small country lane, Yuri in the white van leading our little convoy.

We pull up to the front of a magnificent house resting near the banks of the Oskil river, which is serving as their billet while they are posted here. We walk through the large gates and into a stone slabbed courtyard. Whatever family had previously lived there was clearly one of means.

A tired-looking older soldier stares at us as we come in and stubs out his cigarette while he sits on a little porch that overlooks the river and surrounding area. His gun rests on the chair opposite.

'Cava?'

I go into the little kitchen, where a couple of soldiers are eating, to help him prepare coffee. He speaks no English, but the atmosphere is not awkward. We speak a different language, but we are on the same side.

He whistles while he stirs. The sound of shellfire is constant from the other side of the hill. He seems entirely unperturbed, which I take as a good sign. Then he pauses mid-stir. He stares straight forward at the kitchen cabinet, straining his eyes.

'Ukraini,' he nods. He says it as much to himself as me, then recommences with stirring.

When we are back in the courtyard, he points over the hill to where the firing is coming from.

'Polish crap.'

'No good?' I ask.

'Erm….' He motions Oleg over.

'Polish Crab system.'

'Is it good?'

I wait while Oleg translates and study Yuri's face for a reaction to the question. His cheeks raise, and he smiles broadly. He speaks, and Oleg laughs.

'He says it's fucking amazing,' Oleg translates. The three of us laugh, and Yuri explains the change in the war.

At the beginning of the war, the Ukrainian army and the Russian army were both using the same type of artillery. Soviet. Analog-controlled, inaccurate, and only capable of shooting one shell at a time. It can fire two hundred kilometres, Yuri explains, but it has an accuracy that is so inconsistent that a shell can land anywhere in a two hundred metre radius of where it was aimed. Artillery was a big reason Russia had an initial advantage. They simply had more.

NATO and the West have provided arms and artillery since the start of the invasion. And that addition to the Ukrainian armament is starting to be felt. The Polish crab system shoots three shells at a time. Each is fired at a different trajectory at the same target. Its accuracy is within fifteen metres of where it is aimed. It is modern and electronic. The Germans have provided similar standards of artillery. Other arms have also been given. He talks of the anti-tank rocket launchers. Indeed, the Russians have lost so many tanks that they are now using a model called the T-62. These are tanks that were built over sixty years ago.

They fight like the past, he says. A war of attrition. But this does not have the same impact in modern warfare. It is no longer enough to simply throw men forward and hope that by virtue of numbers alone, you will have success. Times have changed.

'The Russians. They run,' Yuri concludes, waving the back of his hand toward the horizon dismissively. 'They run.'

The light in his eye's wavers only once. When he talks about the many friends he has lost since the start of the war.

You feel the camaraderie the soldiers share, and in the brief exchanges they have, rare is it for them to end on anything other than laughter. It is the brotherhood of the soldier.

When Yuri goes off for a minute, and Oleg and I are alone, Oleg explains the key difference between the war and for the soldiers. For months they fought a defensive war. Now, they are on the offensive. Every day there are advances. It is well known that the Russians are struggling. I ask whether this is simply part of the information war, but Oleg shakes his head. Then he tells me of a common expression among the troops.

'They say, once the Russian army was the second best in the world. Now, it is only the second best in Ukraine.'

We spend another hour or so chatting and go out onto the driveway when we hear a tank. At first, we see nothing. It is shrouded in the forest. Then it emerges, lumbering forward and crossing the Oskil on its way to the front.

Yuri gives me a can of preserved meat as a little souvenir and smiles warmly during our departure. I am exhausted and sore. But neither me, Daniel, nor Oleg can keep the smiles from our faces.

The sun is beginning to set by the time we make it back to Izium and the drive back to Kharkiv. Daniel smokes with one hand on the wheel, and a tank pulls out from the side of the road in front of us. A Ukrainian flag stands taut in the wind at the rear. We listen to more Skofka and some Burla. It feels to me like the perfect way to end the day. A day full of hope. Having seen the destruction, it is odd to feel hopeful, but the Ukrainian people have that impact on me. If they can endure this and stay positive, then I have an obligation to join them.

Two checkpoints out from Izium, and we are pulled over. It is hard to tell the police officer's expression; he wears a balaclava. He chats to Daniel through the window for a minute or two, and Daniel gets out. He is smiling.

He picks up the remains of an old Russian rocket. Oleg joins them, and the three of them talk. I decide to get out of the car. There on the ground, the skeletons of three Russian rockets in the grass. They are nothing more than trophies now.

We draw the attention of a couple of soldiers. One comes across the road; he is smiling before he reaches us. I put out my hand to shake his, but he ignores me and goes straight to Daniel. He takes the rocket from him and unscrews the top of it. Laughing, he pretends to hurl the cap at the ground.

'Bo bach!'

Only when he has an armed missile head does he decide to shake my hand. He speaks a little English and cheerily speaks to me and asks me how I am and how I find Ukraine.

We load the back of the van with the missile and another one (minus the cap) and sound our horns as we pull away. The soldiers and police officers raise their fists and waves us off.

'How does this compare to the last time you were here?' I ask Oleg when we stop for fuel on the way back.

'Oh, totally different ball game. There is no fear in the air.'

The atmosphere, buoyed no doubt by the liberation of Kherson, does seem almost carnival in its nature. The momentum has switched. The war is not over yet, but the soldiers believe. It is clear they believe that their time has come.

I can only imagine how a Russian soldier feels in Ukraine right now.

We are stopped at another checkpoint an hour from Kharkiv. Daniel chats to the soldiers, and the back door opens. A soldier gets into the back. We shake hands, and for a considerable amount of the time on the way back, Daniel and the soldier chat. The roads have improved, and I feel myself falling asleep.

Up ahead, past a treeline maybe ten kilometres away, I spot a flash across the sky. It resembles a shooting star. It is a Russian shell.

'Did you see?' Daniel asks.

'Yes.'

'Russian fascists. Fuck Putin.'

We put the items in the back of the van next to the rockets, and after another round of hugs and handshakes, we leave.

I tip my hat to Oleg and Daniel. By the time we reach the restaurant, they both look like they could sleep standing up. I order more vodka, and perhaps influenced by this, I ask Oleg whether he thinks the Russians will ever stand up and oust Putin.

'When I was here in July and August, I sent my mother some pictures of where I have been. You know what she told me? Those are not real. You got them from the internet. This is not true. She is a Putin loyalist. I think we will not speak in this life again.'

It's a shocking admission. A son's pictures rejected as fake news by his own mother.

Oleg continues by telling me about some of the key issues in Russia that make a general revolt highly unlikely. Russia has painted the West as being morally bankrupt. Many Russians believe that they have the moral high ground. This, he says, had been propagated by propaganda for nearly two decades.

'You think they have been drip-fed propaganda?'

'Yes.'

He then explains the massive police force in Russia, which by official Russian documents, outnumbers the army nearly two to one. This has grown exponentially since Putin came to power. Any protests held would need to be on a scale unimaginable to challenge this police state. Already thousands have been arrested. But it's not those thousands that concern Oleg. It's the hundreds of thousands, by his estimate quite possibly over a million in the last two or three years alone, that concerns him.

'They did not close the borders when the people were leaving. Do you know why?'

I shake my head.

'Because Putin does not care if these people leave. He does not care if Russia is weakened. He only wants those that stay to be loyalists. Some can't leave, of course. But if you don't like it, you can leave. This is the way he thinks. He does not care. This is what the West and even many Ukrainians do not understand.

Russia is just a giant North Korea.'

The sirens sound around ten pm. I don't even leave my bed. Having seen the devastation of the day, I realise that the two-wall rule is likely a fallacy, simply designed to make the population feel safer. I hear a bomb in the distance. I feel the vibrations from it in the hotel room. The siren stops after a while.

Despite my fatigue, I cannot sleep. The day is racing through my mind. So much to try and comprehend. So much to take in. At midnight, I head down the stairs to have a smoke. Julia joins me.

'The sirens.'

'Yes.'

'Do they happen often?'

'Not much. Just sometimes.'

As I take a drag, she says quietly, 'It is so terrible. Many died. Much destroyed. My uncle in Lypsie has had no electricity since twenty-fifth of February. This is all so terrible.'

I cannot see her face as she speaks; the blackout is all-enveloping. This faceless quality gives her words a deeper resonance. Julia does not speak just for Julia. She speaks for many millions of Ukrainians.

November 13th

The day starts later. The unspoken consensus between the three of us was that we all needed a rest after the travails of the day before. Daniel appears at the hotel around ten in the morning, and after a coffee, we go to the garage to fill more food packages for the following day.

As we work, Daniel and Oleg discuss which area we will go to. North is the decision. Kozacha Lopan.

'Very red area,' Daniel says. I recall that it was this village where he had fled under shellfire only two weeks previous.

'How many times have you come under shellfire?'

'The first time I was shelled was in Northern Saltivka, in the six hundred and two district near the medical centre. I saw how people died right there on the spot. I didn't know what to do at that time, so I got into my car and drove away. I did not even think about saving anyone. I was in shock. I was just trying to save my life. During the course of the war, I came under fire six times. Laterally, I knew what to do. I lie on the ground. Cover my important body parts and crawl in the direction of the shelter.'

I give an audible sigh at his response. 'How do you feel? Do you think you've changed?'

'I think I have, of course, changed psychologically quite a bit. Sometimes I can sense that I am more aggressive than before. I think my personality has changed. I hate Russia's army and those who support Russia with all my heart. Glory to Ukraine and its people.'

'Glory to Ukraine.'

It's a beautiful day, and the sun beams in through the open double-doored front of the garage. I strip down to just my thermals.

'Teplo,' I say. Warm. Daniel smiles at my attempts at Ukrainian but nods encouragingly.

After an hour, the siren sounds across the city. Daniel barely acknowledges it, and we work through it without a thought. We stop frequently and drink some more of the tea his mother has made us and chat a little.

'Tired?' I ask him.

'Yes.'

'Long day yesterday.'

'Long months,' he replies.

Months. The endurance and adaptability of the Ukrainian people has been incredible. How much can a country take? I ask Daniel what his hopes are for the future and what he thinks might happen next.

'There's lots of work to be done. And I will continue working, doing what I'm doing, helping people while our organisation is needed. I will deliver aid to people for as long as we are required. As for my plans for the future. I want to work in the building trade and construction business because my father, before he died, was a founder and a big shareholder of a building company, and I want to continue this business. My dream is to help people rebuild their homes free of charge if I have the opportunity. And I also want to work with logistics.'

By the early afternoon, we finish preparing the food bags for the next day. It is the sum of our work for the day. Fatigue can lead to stupid decisions or delayed reactions, and for where we are going tomorrow, Oleg and Daniel make it clear neither of these things is desirable.

Instead, Daniel agrees to take me on a tour of his city to see the worst affected areas. He wants me to understand how Kharkiv has suffered, so he decides to take me to Northern Saltivka.

NORTHERN SALTIVKA

15:42

Even from the road, the scale of damage quickly becomes apparent. We park next to a tower block, blackened and the front of it reduced to a pile of rubble, collecting like scree from a mountain face at the bottom of the building.

I can see into the living rooms and bedrooms of the people who used to live here. Sticks of metal poke out where the concrete used to be attached. In the parts worst damaged, I must shield my eyes against the setting sun which shines through the gaps. Sitting on top of the collection of debris, a small yellow toy car catches my eye, balanced on top of the carnage, all four wheels still attached.

The authorities have attempted to tie up a tarpaulin to cover over the worst of the gashes. It has torn free and flaps in the wind like the flag of an unknown nation.

'Come,' Daniel says and leads us through to the rest of the residential estate. Dozens of tower blocks surround us. All of them bear the same mutilation. 'Civilians. Each block was one thousand people.'

It is a very typical design of the Soviet era. Purpose-built residential blocks of flats with a green space nestled between them. And a nursery.

The walls are cracked, and the windows all blown out. The scorch marks from where the flames licked. The fence around the nursery has little chunks of it blown away. We step through one of the gaps to take a closer look.

On the path that goes around it, sits a little white chair meant for a toddler. It sits alone and empty. What of the little boys and girls who sat on it? Daniel is further around the building and calls to me. He is at the window of the dormitory. Shattered glass glistens in the sun, covering the beds and the floor. There are bouquets of flowers on some of the beds.

Never in my life have I felt a smile so far from my lips. Never has laughter felt more in exile.

It is hard to imagine anyone has survived. That anyone *could* survive in Northern Saltivka. These giant monoliths are no longer homes but towering mausoleums. In the time we are there, we cannot see the full extent of the damage. The area is too vast. The population and size of Northern Saltivka is hard to know and difficult to define. But even the most conservative of estimates put the population of the area at one hundred thousand before the start of the invasion.

As I take a picture of one of the tower blocks, I look up. An elderly woman is staring down at me. She withdraws as soon as I see her.

'There's people still living here?'

'Yes,' Daniel replies. 'No windows. Winter.' He shakes his head.

I take no more photos.

This is not the vision of a civilized world I see before me. Somehow, I find the experience there more harrowing than the day before. The scale of lost life and damage dwarfs many of the villages yesterday. I walk away from Oleg and Daniel and wander alone for a while.

***

'War is too often looked at through statistics,' Oleg says. 'Northern Saltivka is terrible, of course. But two dozen die in the village, and maybe that village never recovers. The cities, at least, will recover. But numbers aren't stories. It's math. Not stories.'

Stories. That is war. This is Ukraine. Millions of people, their stories intertwined with happenings out of their control and that they had no part in creating. Each carries their sorrow. Each has a story unique to themselves. Each deserves respect for what they have been through. Villager. Urbanite. All are interconnected with the pain and suffering caused by this invasion.

I recognise that Oleg is correct. Many of the villages and towns we saw yesterday I can never imagine being rebuilt. I hope I am mistaken. Perhaps one day, I will return to see these places again, and I hope they are recovered. The other thing that blows my mind is that I haven't seen even the tip of the iceberg. There will be countless villages and towns across Ukraine that are in similar states.

'The main thing is this. The international community must not stop or slacken with their support. Ukraine is winning, but there can be no complacency. The numbers might tell them it is ok to slow down.'

Back in Kharkiv, we visit one of the many military stores in the city. There is a plethora of military goods. Boots. Knives. Jackets. Trousers. Night vision goggles. Guns. The selection is overwhelming.

Oleg picks out a winter jacket, not unlike Daniels, and a pair of boots. Daniel buys a balaclava. When we leave the shop, which is part of a much bigger complex, an air raid siren sounds. It echoes off the cavernous walls and reverberates around the whole of the mall. Not one person stops what they are doing. Only me. I stop and look up. The war has become a normality. The air raid sirens just another part of daily life.

The siren goes off again later that night. Three large explosions occur in the West of the city. I fall asleep to it ringing in my ears.

November 14th

We take the road North out of Kharkiv and through a settlement. Down the side of the road for a kilometre or more are signs with pictures of people and their names written underneath. They are the faces of ghosts.

KOZACHA LOPAN

08:02

A man in an LA Lakers hat approaches us. There is blood down the front of his top. The knee on one of his trousers legs is gone. He asks me for a cigarette. I oblige, and we smoke together. He speaks to Oleg and Daniel and tells them his story. It has been a tough few months in Kozacha Lopan. At the end of my cigarette, I decided to give him the remainder of the packet. He thanks me. We give him a food package as well, and then he disappears back into the village, past the ruin of a house.

A woman with gold for teeth comes to us a couple of minutes later. She speaks little and takes the food package with barely a smile. 'Spasiba,' she says quietly.

We are parked outside the administrative building for the village. It must be dark inside; the sandbags are stacked so high.

I have never seen so many sandbags. There must be thousands. We have arrived too early. There are no officials in the building yet, and few locals are around. Oleg and Daniel walk around, trying to see if they can get anyone's attention.

Oleg spots a table outside the building. Sitting on it, the parts of a destroyed drone. The charred lens, the fragmented engine. On the ground in front of it is a Russian flag. There is no expression on his face. He picks up the flag, and after a few failed attempts, he lights a corner of it and lets it burn.

'This is twenty years back in Russia. I guess I won't be back.'

We leave Kozacha Lopan and drive around, looking through these lost villages for signs of life and people we can help.

At a crossroads, a local man calls out to Daniel. After a brief exchange, the man gets in the back of the car and gives directions to find his village.

SHEVCHENKA

08:16

I suppose what we are driving on was once a road. Clumps of weeds and grass have engulfed it. There are glimpses of gravel and a ditch at the side which hasn't quite been overrun. The windows of the houses we pass are misty with condensation.

To my surprise, the village still has electricity, the man says. Even prior to the war, it looks like a place that might have been without.

The ring of our vehicle's horns abruptly breaks the early morning silence. The man jumps out, without even waiting for the car to come to a full stop, puts his hands to his mouth, and shouts. He moves off toward a three-story house, hollering and clapping. Daniel waits at the wheel patiently.

'That is Russia,' Oleg says, pointing at a field past the row of houses just in front of us. Four hundred metres away is the border. Oleg gets his phone to take a photo. He stalls with it still in his hand and stares at the screen. There is a tight smile on his face. He turns the phone so that I can read the message he has just received from EE.

"Welcome to Russia."

The man returns a few minutes later with a couple of people. One of the women joins his chorus, and other villagers slowly begin to appear. It is nothing like Borova. No stream of people. The situation here is desperate. But they are afraid. It is obvious. I see a couple of curtains twitch in the houses opposite us.

Oleg explains why they are so tentative. They stay in their homes. The drones come by often. He tells me to keep my eyes on the skies whenever I have a chance. Shells could come at any time, and we are well within the mortar range of Russia.

The drones come in two different styles. Those that kill with rockets. And those that spot people for the mortars and artillery to kill.

A man approaches on crutches. His wears a pair of old, ill-fitting adidas shoes. He squelches through the mulch of leaves, damp from the thawing frost. His right ankle is at a queer angle. He takes a bag, says nothing, and stumbles away.

An older man, talkative and in better health, talks to Oleg and Daniel. He is emotional. Most people only get one bag to ensure we can reach as many people as possible. Oleg gives the man two, and the man hugs him.

'Why did he get two?' I ask once he has walked away.

'He is seventy-five years old. So is his wife. A bomb landed near her, and she got shell shock. She is deaf now. They have been married over fifty years and now.' Oleg shrugs. 'He needs two.'

Two ladies embrace next to us with tears in their eyes. They talk for a short time, then split off and go in opposite directions.

'They might not have seen each other for weeks. Everyone is afraid to leave their homes.'

More people gather. Some walk toward us at a leisurely pace. Others, regardless of age, charge toward us. One woman in her late fifties, or early sixties, breezes past four people half her age. She is breathing hard by the time she reaches us. She leans on me, puffing her cheeks. We give her two bags. She says her partner is at home.

The poverty in Shevchenka is almost tangible. Here, people do not live. They exist.

The mood, however, is quite pleasant. Some of the villagers chat together, and for a time, they seem relaxed. Then a woman waiting for a food package speaks. The group turns silent. She can hear a drone. All eyes are averted toward the sky to see if anyone can spot the angel of death.

I can't hear anything, but a couple of the other villagers claim that they can. We hand out food packages to the remaining villagers, and the crowd quickly disperses. They go back to hiding.

KOZACHA LOPAN
09:04

Daniel stops the car at a checkpoint and speaks with the soldiers. They confirm that the administrative building is open in Kozacha Lopan.

Straight away, Oleg and Daniel manage to get the attention of a couple of the locals. We make contact with one of the officials who points towards a large parking bay in front of a burnt-out building. We drive over, and a few of the locals gather and shout into the village.

The queue forms more quickly. The people are more at ease. Kozacha Lopan feels different from Shevchenka. The people speak freely to Oleg and Daniel, and there is more laughter. A few of them try to speak with me. One man looks at me incredulously.

'Britanski!' He looks astonished and shakes my hand vociferously.

I am taking a photo of Oleg and Daniel with a few of the people we have given food packages to when we hear artillery. I lower the camera and look off toward Russia, which is still easily within sight. Oleg and Daniel unfreeze from their poses and speak to the locals, Daniel still with his arm around the woman who was next to him for the picture. They are speaking hurriedly, the syllables overlapping as one villager interrupts another.

'They say it's Ukrainian,' Oleg says.

These villagers have been turned into army veterans by the war. They can hear drones and the difference in sound between

Ukrainian and Russian artillery. They know it can be the difference between life and death. And so does Daniel.

'Daniel knows how this gig goes,' Oleg says,' they will fire back in five minutes.'

'Artillery answering artillery.'

'Yes. Exactly. An explosive conversation!'

The proceedings quicken in pace, and now the people taking the food packages say nothing; they simply grab the bags and dart back into the village where they hope they'll be safer. There is no guarantee, of course. They may be simply running toward where the next shell is going to plant itself. There is no way of telling. As Oleg says, it's just luck who lives and who dies.

'Bystro! Bystro!' Daniel says, hurrying the last couple of people. He takes a bag to an older woman that we can see coming from the end of the street.

When we see that no more villagers are coming, we pack up the vehicles and drive back to the administrative building a few hundred metres down the road. Daniel is keen to get the contact details. Points of contact are essential for navigating aid drop-offs. They may also have good information about the surrounding area. It feels like you could drive through this part of Ukraine for a year and still fail to see every one of the numerous villages.

I am tense. Oleg and I wait in the cars outside. I strain my ears for the sound of shelling and look into the sky for drones. A woman crosses the street and knocks at my window. I lower it, and she begins speaking to me. I point her over to Oleg. She quickly understands. I can guess by the two empty boxes of medicine she is clutching in her hand what she needs. One box is painkillers. The other medicine is for arthritis.

She passes the boxes to Oleg through the window, and they talk for a moment.

'Spasiba!' She calls out before walking briskly down a side street.

Daniel re-emerges from the sandbagged entrance a few minutes later, and without even putting on his seatbelt, we pull away. We drive down the same road we used to enter Kozacha Lopan, but this time a little faster than before.

After driving for a few minutes, we spot a dozen Ukrainian soldiers at the side of the road. They are wandering around a couple of fresh craters that are only five minutes old. The time it took Daniel inside the administrative building. I'm not religious, but it feels like divine intervention.

I breathe a little easier for every kilometre we put between ourselves and Kozacha Lopan and Shevchenka. For months they have lived in this limbo.

'Why do you think they bomb Kozacha Lopan and places like it?'

'I don't know,' Daniel says. 'Here is just civilians. No military. No one here is fighting. It is a kind of sickness. Madness.'

We turn down a small dirt road. The houses to the left of us are obliterated. The ones on the right-hand side are remarkably untouched. We park seven houses down. Daniel gets out and chaps a big metal door.

A stout man with a big fuzzy salt and pepper beard and a flat cap opens the door. He cries out and hugs Daniel and Oleg, and me. He wears a beaming smile; white teeth gleam from between the follicle forest.

He walks us into the yard. There are a dozen dogs. They create a terrible racket, but they are friendly and come and sniff us, their tails wagging. He chats amiably with Oleg and Daniel, gesturing with his hand and smiling. Always smiling. It's incredible to find someone so happy in this place.

His home has been destroyed. He lives with his neighbours now, whose courtyard we are standing in. He limps slightly and slaps the back of his right thigh, where he was hit by a piece of shrapnel. I am busy with one of the dogs when Oleg calls me over to them. He's found out I'm Scottish. He gives me a big thumbs up and says something to Oleg. He waits while Oleg translates, his eyebrows dancing while he stares at me.

'He says the Scottish are a good ancient people.' The man adds to this, and Oleg chuckles. 'They fight the English.'

'We still do.' Oleg translates my response, and the three of us laugh. He comes over and holds me in a tight embrace.

When he withdraws, he puts up his right arm and flexes it. He urges me to touch his bicep. I put my hand on it.

'Strong man!'

He points once more to his arm, where my hand still rests, and then points to the front of his trousers. He speaks and laughs.

Oleg grins as he translates, 'big arm. Big balls.'

He then tries to speak a bit of French to me. When he sees I lack comprehension, he breaks into a rendition of Edith Paif, lifting his finger in time with the movement of his Adam's apple.

Some people don't need language to tell you the type of person they are.

Daniel has been to this man a few times. I recognise him from a video that Daniel took and posted on the Sunflower Scotland youtube channel. Daniel leaves for a moment and retrieves a couple of food packages which the man accepts very gratefully. He goes down to the bottom of the courtyard and returns with a huge bushel of apples which he insists we take. Oleg and I still have it in the back of the van when we get to Edinburgh.

We leave to hugs and back slaps. He doffs his flat cap and waves it at us when we leave. He shouts after us until we are out of earshot.

***

We meander through a few more villages. We have a few bags left, not many. There is no plan to take them back to Kharkiv, so I'm deployed as a spotter.

We see a few men gathered on a street corner, all of them over the age of sixty, I would guess. They are having a chat, and when we pull alongside them, they stop and look at us. Daniel asks them how their conditions are. Their response needs no translation. We open the back of the van and give them all a food package.

One of the men has Oleg's ear and is chatting to him incessantly. Oleg pats the man on the shoulder and nods with a sad look on his face. The man wipes his face free of tears. Later in the day, Oleg explains to me that the man was very lonely.

In the next village, we give our final bag to a babooshka at the side of the road. She looks impossibly old. Her face so tight with wrinkles that her eyes peep out from behind the multiple folds of her skin. She holds my hand tight and starts to moan to me in Ukrainian. She is very upset. I can tell from Daniel and Oleg's faces that her story is sad. She has endured many hardships, and her family has gone. Daniel tells me that she is tired and miserable with the war and too old to be bothered with it. She just wants peace. She takes our bag and walks down the ditch to the back of her house.

Daniel removes the flask from the car and steps out. He beckons for me to follow. We are sat next to a big white house. I can see over the fence that the two outhouses have been destroyed by shelling. Oleg clambers out of the van and joins us next to the gate. Then Daniel produces a key and opens the gate.

'Your house?'

'Yes. My house.' He points at the rubble. 'Two months ago. Russian fascists. I think that the reason why I want to help people rebuild their homes because I know first-hand how it feels to have your home attacked by a missile. I know how it feels. I want to help people as much as I can to rebuild their lives.'

The house itself is largely untouched, though the windows were smashed in the blast and are now boarded over.

'My father build.'

'Wow. Good job.'

'Yes. Good job.'

He puts his flask on the garden table, and we have some tea and biscuits. We wander idly through the wreckage. It feels odd. These buildings, or what remains of them, belong to my friend. There is no anonymity to this destruction; there is a name attached. He shakes his head every so often, and Oleg and he talks in short staccato sentences.

Over the garden fence, a field stretches out toward a small grove of trees, and the sun reflects off the surface of a little river that snakes down the hill. The landscape is flat, and from this vantage point, I can see through the haze the vast extended virgin landscape stretching out to the horizon.

Once we're finished, he gives us a guided tour of his home. The interior of the house is blanketed in darkness, and we use our torches to light the way. It's a lovely home, with spacious rooms and a big kitchen in the back with a door that leads onto a wooden veranda. We head up the stairs to his old bedroom, where the walls are still plastered with posters from his youth. I sometimes forget that he is still in his youth.

He walks over to the bookcase and fingers through the spines before pulling one of them out. It's a book on English grammar, written in English. He hands it to me and smiles.

'For you.'

'Thanks?'

'Subtle trolling,' Oleg says with a grin.

Also sitting on that bookcase is a picture of him with his father, who died in 2014. The pair of them smile back at me, Daniel's arm resting on his father's shoulder.

We sit in Ottantotto 88 and have a couple of drinks while we eat. Aware that this is our last dinner together, I ask Daniel a few questions that have been pressing on my mind.

'When the war started, where were you? What was your first impression? What were the actions you took?'

'I went to fuel up as quickly as I could because we didn't understand what was happening. I was very worried. People were scared. We didn't know what would happen next.'

'When you realised they had invaded, what did you do?'

'I went to the drafting office to join the army, but it was closed. There was a sign that I should go to the tank academy, which I did. When I went to tank academy, there was soldiers there in uniform who had served before. They took my details and said that someone would be in touch with me. However, nobody called.'

'I have been wanting to ask that. Why haven't you joined the army? Was their pressure from your mother not to?'

'Yes. At first, my mum was very afraid. I am her only son. But I found my purpose in helping people, and I have been helping people ever since. I think it's very important, very necessary. This is the reason I haven't joined the army.'

I nod. 'What do you think about the thousands, if not hundreds of thousands of Russians, who do not agree with the war? Do you feel a connection to them?'

He pauses for a moment before he replies and sighs deeply. 'When we had a bad president, Ukrainians went out and overthrew the bad president because we are a strong people. In Russia, they don't do it. So what's my attitude? My attitude is that I don't like those people in Russia. Why are they not helping Ukraine? They should leave the country and start helping Ukraine. My opinion of them is bad. I think they are bad people.'

'Thank you, Daniel. Thank you for taking us around Kharkiv and the frontline villages and towns. Thank you for being honest and sharing with me.'

We clink our glasses together.

'Slava Ukraini.'

'Any man who thinks he has the right to challenge whether people exist or not, that thinks he has the right to kill, seeks to take the place of God.'

Oleg and I are having a cup of tea in the hotel after dinner when he tells me this. He expands on the point he is making between sips. 'Putin is a return to the days of the tsar,' he explains, 'to an absolute monarchy which, historically, were believed to have a direct line to God. This is the mantel that Putin has dusted off and placed himself upon. It's at the stage where priests in the Russian Orthodox Church have been videoed blessing bombs. This is why he does not care if people leave. He wants only the believers in him. The almighty.

Through steady propaganda and Russia's development into a police state, he has elevated himself to the position where he is no longer just a man. He is everything. He is Russia. He is their protector. He is divine. And many Russians have fallen for the allure of this false idol. He has painstakingly painted himself as the saviour. The one to follow.'

I take some time to digest these thoughts. They are dark and troubling and point to a society so lost that I don't know how it finds itself again.

'I think he has become a God, Oleg. The God of death.'

November 15th

KHARKIV

08:36

Daniel comes to the hotel to see us off before we leave. I am saying my goodbye to Julia when he arrives. She sits timidly behind the reception desk. 'Thank you,' she says.

I will confess I struggle not to lose myself to emotion on that final morning. It is an odd feeling to be so bound to someone who had been a stranger only a week before.

As we say our goodbyes in the foyer, some soldiers filter past us with their guns. This is the true nature of war. It relentlessly permeates every part of daily life. The hotels have become barracks. Towns and villages have become graveyards. There is no peace. There is no escape. There are reminders at every moment.

I look forward to coming back when the sandbags are gone. The soldiers no longer present. The air silent of sirens. My hand no longer poised for my passport. The power cuts desisted. When we no longer spend our dinners in the evenings discussing what impoverished town we should visit the following day. When families no longer cower and grieve with the question of "who's next?" hanging over them.

How much sadness can a country take? As much as is required, and the Ukrainians have risen to the challenge of tyranny with heart.

They still need our support. The war is not over yet, and, unfortunately, I fear many people will die before it does. But I have met a proud people. A country unbroken despite Russia's best efforts. A people who have nothing but my eternal gratitude and respect.

***

We pass through a checkpoint on the outskirts of the city, past the fuel station where we met Daniel for the first time. The sun is coming up, blue hue over deep orange.

'Where are we picking up Hanna in Kyiv?'

'We will pick her up at a fuel station.'

Hanna is the mother of Tanya, one of the committee members of Sunflower Scotland. With the onset of winter and no cessation in the bombing of infrastructure and civilians, she has decided to leave.

'Alright.'

'Now you have seen, huh?'

As we drive back down the E40, I put my pen and notepad back into my bag and sit leaning against the window. I watch the countryside pass and fall asleep.

When I wake, we are approaching Kyiv. I look down at my phone.

Telegram message 16:05 Daniel – Strong arrivals in Kharkiv. Already three times.

Telegram message 16:06 Daniel – Already five.

Telegram message 16:07 Daniel – The light is gone.

I message him back but get no reply. I am still waiting for one when we pull into the gas station. I notice that it is closed, which strikes me as strange.

A woman in a little pink woollen hat comes over to us. She is smiling. It is Hanna. We get out and give her a hand with her luggage. She speaks quickly to Oleg, who immediately looks concerned.

'She didn't see it, but two rockets flew over the gas station only a few minutes ago.'

Once she is safely in the backseat and her luggage put away, I take out my phone and look at the news. It is then we are made aware that the whole of Ukraine is under missile attack—the largest missile attack since the war began.

For the next few minutes, I am in shock. Two of the rockets hit a residential district less than a kilometre from the gas station, and I can hear the sirens of emergency vehicles. Oleg and Hanna talk to one another. Hanna's phone rings, and she takes a call.

As of writing this, there are two confirmed deaths from the strikes on the tower blocks. Likely it is more. I can practically hear Daniel next to me whispering, 'Civilians.'

Half an hour outside Kyiv, I'm relieved when he calls Oleg. The power is out, he confirms, but he is ok. They are ok. He is with his girlfriend and mother. They have a generator and some gas. They will be ok.

Zhytomyr

19:06

We are trying to ascertain whether Zhytomyr still has problems with power by looking into people's windows as we pass their homes. Most seem to have no power. Oleg makes the decision that if the hotel has no power, we will make for Poland tonight.

It is easily another few hours to Poland, and goodness knows the situation on the border. We wind down the narrow streets, Oleg flicking the fog light off and on to avoid blinding drivers coming in the opposite direction. I am not hopeful.

I recognise the old church and breathe a sigh of relief when I catch sight of the bright lights of the hotel. It might be the only building we've passed for the last mile that has electricity. Oleg takes his time parking, takes the key out of the ignition, and slumps forward over the steering wheel.

I slap him on the shoulder, 'That was quite the drive.'

He sighs and nods with his head hung low, the glare of the hotel down one side of his face and catching the glass of his spectacles. 'Yes. Yes, it was.'

Our suspicions are confirmed by the receptionist, who informs us that Zhytomyr is experiencing a complete blackout. The hotel has only been spared by its numerous generators. When I get into my room and drop off my bags, I sit momentarily on the edge of my bed and put my head in my hands. I am extremely fatigued. The type of fatigue that is insidious. It brings a sadness. The day's events and all I have witnessed are catching up with me.I go to the bathroom. I splash cold water on my face and go back downstairs before I can think any further about it.

Oleg and Hanna already have a table. Hanna is gesturing to the waiter with her hands. He shakes his head and leaves the table.

'What was that all about?'

'He says the kitchen is closed.'

'Shit.'

'Hanna convinced him otherwise.'

I smile at her and give a feeble thumbs up.

After some dinner and wine, the three of us sit at the table in near silence. I am scoping through the news on my phone, desperate to keep updated with developments. Oleg stares into space. Hanna has a conversation on her phone.

I have a mouthful of wine which nearly ends up all over the cream tablecloth when I read the breaking news.

"Russian missiles hit Poland."

'Holy shit.'

'I'm not surprised,' Oleg says. 'They've been playing with fire for months now.

'If NATO does nothing…' Oleg raises a weary hand and lets it drop. 'So weak. Close the sky. This is the chance to do something active about it. Ukrainian or Russian missile, it does not matter. It hit an EU country, a member of NATO, directly because of the war started by Russia. If we appease Russia now and let it off the hook, then I think I don't know what the purpose of NATO is. Maybe Putin has bought a nice house at Lake Como for this Stoltenberg. Corruption is everywhere.'

'Oh my god.'

I quickly message a couple of my friends with the news. I get gobsmacked responses and sit back in my seat. The rest of the glass of wine is gone in a single gulp.

'Is this war?'

'As I say. Close the sky. It has needed to happen from the beginning.' Oleg gives a tired shrug.

He and Hanna speak for a few minutes while I scroll madly and open new tabs searching for news.

Two Poles dead on the farm hit by the missile. An attack on a member of NATO. Then the reports begin of the missile potentially being a Ukrainian one. Oleg asks for the bill. I finish the glass of wine, turn off my phone and decide I will not look at it for the rest of the night.

November 16th

As soon as I wake up, I check my phone. Throughout the night, there have been discussions about where the missile came from. Whether it was Ukrainian or Russian. Poland has called for article five. This is the first step toward NATO taking military action.

I take a quick shower. It is clear from Oleg's face at the reception that he has already read the news.

'They will do nothing.' He sighs heavily. 'Already there is the talk. Was it Ukrainian? Was it Russian? At what point does our inaction become an accessory?'

I continually rotate between three news sources as we drive toward the Polish border. BBC, Reuters, and Al-Jazeera. I read to Oleg as he drives. More reports are emerging of evidence that the missile is Ukrainian. Poland backpedals from its initial request for a meeting.

'Think of all we have seen, David. Saltivka. The villages and towns. Think of the coming winter. People will die. I think maybe, some of that blood is on our hands if we do nothing. We must close the skies. It is sick to think of it this way, but this is the opportunity we have waited for—the opportunity to do something more. Close the skies. It is not direct conflict, but something must be done.'

The mood is solemn in the car. He and Hanna speak infrequently. She has a phone call with her daughter, who is meeting her in Krakow. Other than that, it is complete silence.

We are only a hundred kilometres from the border when Daniel calls. The crossing we were planning to take into Poland has been closed. It is the region where the missiles landed. We pull into a Wog while Oleg ponders what to do next. He scours through the GPS. It begins to rain as I stand outside smoking. It is the first time it has rained since we have been in Ukraine.

Oleg elects to go North and enter Poland through Lutsk. When I get back in, he taps the new directions into the screen and grimly pulls out from the petrol station. An hour later, we arrive in Rivne.

It takes me a few moments to realise it is Rivne. I have been here before. Five years ago, I was here with my partner Viktoria. It feels like a lifetime ago. I see the small shisha shack on the riverbank where we sat on the beanbags outside and shared a pipe with her friend Sasha and her partner Sergei.

***

Oleg and Hanna are speaking in hurried words. They speak loudly while Oleg gestures toward the long queue of traffic waiting at the border crossing. It stretches at least a couple of kilometres. He relents, pulls out of the jam, and drives on the other side of the road toward the checkpoint. There is no traffic moving in the opposite direction.

We come to a halt as the the armed border guards motion towards us and signal us to turn around. Two other cars are already u-turning, and my heart sinks at the prospect of the long wait. The car is still moving when Hanna slides open the side door and starts berating them. She unclips her seatbelt and takes a couple of steps out of the car. Reluctantly a young man comes forward to look at our papers and passports. Hanna is still speaking and pointing behind us when they take hers.

They tell Oleg to turn off the engine and take the keys. Then they disappear into a hut at the side of the road.

A few minutes later, the border guards return and speak to Oleg. He nods, and they stamp our passports.

'Spasiba.'

'What's happening?'

'They are letting us through. We just have to wait a few minutes.'

'Really? How?'

'Always have a Ukrainian woman on your side.'

It is a bittersweet moment when we cross over into Poland. I feel a great sense of relief and message people to let them know we have left Ukraine. But my thoughts are to those that can't leave.

We pass through Poland, unmolested by bombing and destruction, but I keep searching all the same, a reflex spawned by our experiences of the last week.

I tell Oleg of this, as we are nearing the German border the following day. He smirks, 'Oh, none here. Not yet,' he says casually.

In order to remember, there are some things we must forget.

Forget the idea that Ukraine is some dirt-poor country.
Forget the claim that a good intention is good enough.
Forget the statistics that make war more palatable.
Forget the snippets of information we are given by the media.

Remember, if you want to help Ukraine, to buy Ukrainian.
Remember the millions of people and their unique stories.
Remember the towns and villages that could easily be forgotten.
Remember Ukraine's suffering and that it has suffered for us to battle fascism.
Remember that you can make a difference.

Afterword

EDINBURGH, MARCH 2023

I'm cold. Oleg has that same grim expression that I got used to in Ukraine, somewhere between a smile and a curse. He delivers the news and sits back in his seat. I take a long drink of beer.

For some time, though it is hard to know exactly how long, Daniel has been inflating figures and embezzling money from the charity.

'I'm heartbroken', Oleg says. His hand shakes slightly. He shifts in his seat. As recently as two weeks before he was in Ukraine. He saw Daniel. Even then, he was unsure of deceit, but certain behaviours made him suspicious.

The most recent trip also spelled trouble of a different nature. It was Oleg's fifth time out to Ukraine, driving there and back, and the strain has taken its toll. He has severe back pain caused by two disks that have herniated.

I look at my friend, moving from side to side awkwardly in his chair, the level of his discomfort all too clear.

'Shit', is the only reply I can muster. I can't believe it and immediately run through possible reasons for why this news can't be true.

Any flames of doubt are doused as Oleg lays bare the bitter reality. Aside from being a driven character, Oleg is beyond conscientious. Documents and invoices, everything is kept.

I do not feel shame for admitting I shed a tear or two as he reels off and shows me where the fraud has taken place.

'It came to a head on the 23rd of March, less than a week ago. We sent Daniel £4100 to purchase 450 food rations for the month. Shortly after, we learned that he was inflating prices for some time. Also, some food was missing from deliveries. We asked him to return our money. He refused and has never shown where this money went.'

'How much do you think?'

'It is hard to say. Thousands maybe. Certainly, something substantial for us. We are not big like Red Cross or something, millions coming in. This was a lot. Any is too much. But this is a lot. I am heartbroken,' he repeats, 'so shocked.'

We are silent for some time. He shuffles across and scrolls through his phone. There is more than enough to condemn Daniel. I feel no anger. Just deep sadness.

Perhaps it was inherently in Daniel's nature to do such a thing. Perhaps he was broken by the war. Regardless, I sense that all the good work he has done with Sunflower, all the sacrifice and risk, has been undermined. We were on the same team, and he left us.

If Daniel had needed to leave and bow out due to the stress of the war, he might only have said. Not one person in the organisation would have thought ill of him for it. The support they gave, whether through the supply of the Mitsubishi four by four, or the body armour and helmet. The fact that Oleg went out there personally on numerous occasions to help him. It was second to none. All they asked for in return, was trust. And this, like any desperate situation of its kind, demands trust. One cannot change a situation so dire, without the help of others.

The trust that I had witnessed between them in Ukraine, I now see dissolve in a small bar in Edinburgh. We spend some time together and drink more than we should, sometimes descending back into silence and our own thoughts. I watch as Oleg leaves the table to go and use the bathroom, lugging his left leg and filtering through the people gauchely.

Oleg has given financially, emotionally and finally, physically everything to Ukraine. He never asks for plaudits. He never asks for recognition. His focus is simple. Help people in need.

To that end, this book isn't about Oleg. It isn't about Daniel, and it certainly isn't about me. It's about the people who suffer. And Sunflower is not an organisation to be dissuaded so easily from this cause.

Since Daniel's fraud, they have moved on. They started working with other Ukrainian volunteers. They have helped deliver food to Kherson and medicines to those directly affected by the blowing up of the Kakhovka dam. They have delivered four by fours to the Ukrainian reservists battling in Bakhmut. Elvira, Oleg's wife, drove an ambulance to Kharkiv Oblast. They have helped frontline medics in Zaporizhzhia repair four ambulances.

In a strange twist of fate, the misfortune with Daniel has energised Sunflower Scotland and proved to be a catalyst in making them a bigger and more far-reaching charity.

They still help the weak. They still help the wounded. And with a resolve and perseverance that I can't help but applaud.

Kyiv, 9th of November

Motherland Monument Kyiv, 9th of November

Hospital in Chuhuiv, 10th of November

Vilkhivka, 10th of November

Vilkhivka, 10th of November

One of the warehouses at the wholesalers in Kharkiv,
11th of November

Kupiansk, 12th of November

Kurylivska, 12th of November

One of the many destroyed Russian tanks we saw on the road to Izium, 12th of November

Yatskivka, 12th of November

Delivery of food aid to Borova, 12th of November. (Oleg, front left. Daniel, front right)

Northern Saltivka, 13th of November

They say the devil is in the detail. This is a close up shot of the debris at the bottom of the tower in the previous photo. Northern Saltivka, 13th of November

Nursery dormitory in Northern Saltivka, 13th of November

Northern Saltivka, 13th of November

Shevchenka, 14th of November

Kozacha Lopan, 14th of November

Zhytomyr, 15th of November

About the Author

David Kenneth Weir Sharkey is a native of Edinburgh, a city steeped in literature. He is a waiter in a mash potato restaurant, who enjoys reading and writing. Influenced by easygoing writers, such as Cormac McCarthy, J G Ballard and Hemingway, David dabbled with the idea of writing a children's book for years. But instead, he ended up going to Ukraine and writing a book about the atrocities of the ongoing war.

He still serves mash. Plays with his son. And spends time with his wife and friends. Every so often, he reads and writes.

"Remember" is his inaugural effort at nonfiction writing and the first piece to be published.

Printed in Great Britain
by Amazon